W9-AXW-430

First Edition

www.apcompsciprinciples.com

Yellow Dart Publishing
2690 Addison Dr.
Doraville, GA 30340

Microsoft product screenshots used with permission from Microsoft

Adobe product screenshots reprinted with permission from Adobe Systems Incorporated.

Adobe®, Adobe® Dreamweaver®, and Adobe® Photoshop are either registered trademarks or trademarks of Adobe Systems Incorporated in the United States and/or other countries.

Google and the Google logo are registered trademarks of Google Inc., used with permission

AP® and Advanced Placement® are trademarks registered by the College Board, which was not involved in the production of, and does not endorse, this text.

ISBN: 9781521137451

Computer Science Principles

About AP® Computer Science Principles

Course Description

CS Principles is a course that exposes students to the beauty and awe of computer science. The course teaches students programming while emphasizing problem solving and logic development. Other topics explored in this course are the impact of computer science and the use of computational tools in data analysis. Students are taught to use computer tools to solve problems pertaining to computer science. Most projects are open-ended and students will be working on them either in pairs or by themselves. As students create projects, they will be asked to narrate the project as well as reflect on their work by writing reports or responding to prompts.

Course Goals and Learning Outcomes

The course is focused around seven big ideas:

- Big Idea 1: **Creativity**—Computing is a creative activity.
- Big Idea 2: **Abstraction**—Abstraction reduces information and detail to facilitate focus on relevant concepts.
- Big Idea 3: **Data and Information**—Data and information facilitate creation of knowledge.

- Big Idea 4: **Algorithms**—Algorithms are used to develop and express solutions to computational problems.
- Big Idea 5: **Programming**—Programming enables problem solving, human expression, and creation of knowledge.
- Big Idea 6: **The Internet**—The Internet pervades modern computing.
- Big Idea 7: **Global Impact**—Computing has global impact.

Each of the ideas is paired with one or more of the following Computational Thinking Practices:

- Connecting Computing
- Creating Computational Artifacts
- Abstracting
- Analyzing Problems and Artifacts
- Communicating Collaborating

Source:

AP Computer Science Principles Course Description
Copyright © 2016 The College Board.
Reproduced with permission.
http://apcentral.collegeboard.com.

Readings, Material, and Resources

- **<u>Blown to Bits: Your Life, Liberty, and Happiness After the Digital Explosion</u>**

  Harold Abelson, Ken Ledeen, Harry Lewis - Addison-Wesley - 2008

- **<u>Nine Algorithms That Changed the Future: The Ingenious Ideas That Drive Today's Computers</u>**

  John MacCormick - Princeton University Press - 2013

- Microsoft Excel® *(Version 15.32)*
- Microsoft Word® *(Version 15.32)*
- Adobe® Photoshop *(2015.5.1 Release)*
- Adobe® Dreamweaver® *(2015.5.1 Release)*
- A Cloud Based Digital Portfolio (i.e. - <u>Google Drive</u>)

Free Software Alternatives

- FreeOffice - http://www.freeoffice.com/ (For Excel and Word)
- GIMP - https://www.gimp.org/ (For Photoshop)
- Brackets - http://brackets.io/ (For Dreamweaver)

Unit 1 – The Computer: Basics and Binary

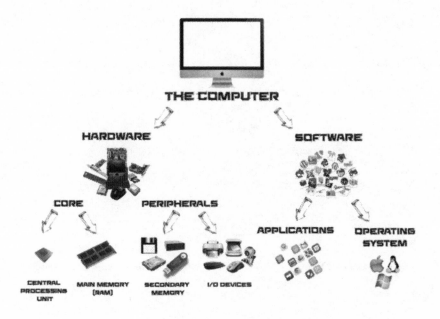

Computers

A **computer** is defined as an electronic device that processes data according to a set of instructions or commands, known as a program. Anyone who has ever turned on a phone or surfed the Internet has used a computer and should have a basic understanding of what happens when the mouse is clicked or the screen is touched (and how fast it happens!). Before creating spreadsheets, manipulating images, understanding the Internet, making website, encrypting data, or learning how to code, it is important to understand the basics of every computer. Desktops, laptops, tablets, and smartphones all convert data into 1's and 0's and all have the same basic components: software and hardware.

Software

The **software** of the computer is just a series of ones and zeros at the lowest level and cannot physically be touched and is usually stored on the hard drive of the computer. The software can be broken down into two general categories: the operating system and the applications.

Operating System

The **operating system** is the visual representation of the computer. The OS includes the desktop, start menu, icons, file view, etc. Again, the software is just a series of ones and zeros that cannot be understood by a human (there are usually billions of them at a time), so the operation systems help make those ones and zeros easy to read and understand. Some popular operating systems include Windows 10, MacOS Sierra, and Linux.

Applications

All other programs on the computer would be considered **applications**. This includes word processors, photo editing software, web browsers, games, music programs, pretty much everything else on your computer except for saved files. A few popular applications include Microsoft Word, Excel, PowerPoint, Adobe Photoshop, Apple iTunes, Google Chrome, and Minecraft.

Hardware

Hardware includes the physical parts of the computer— devices such as the monitor, keyboard, speakers, wires, chips, cables, plugs, disks, printers, mice, and many other items that **can** physically be touched. There are two categories of hardware that each contain two parts: the **core** (the central processing unit (CPU) and the main memory) and the **peripherals** (the input and output (I/O) devices and the secondary memory).

Core

The **core** of a computer consists of the **CPU** and the **main memory**. Together these things do all the "heavy lifting" in the computer. Everything that happens on the computer goes through the core.

Central Processing Unit

The **Central Processing Unit (CPU)** is the part that carries out every command or process on the computer. It can be thought of as the brain of the computer and is extremely fast (usually measured in gigahertz or billions of processes a second). By the time information gets to the CPU it is broken down to all ones and zeros. One of the reasons it can process so many commands is because it only needs to recognize those two numbers.

Main Memory

The **main memory** is the memory that temporarily stores information while it is being sent to the CPU. It also helps break down the information to something the CPU can easily understand. Main memory can be thought of as "the bouncer" of the core, everything that happen goes through the main memory first. The main memory is often referred to as **RAM, or random access memory**. In other words, the memory can be retrieved or written to anywhere in the memory—the computer does not have to go through all the information in the memory to get to the information at the very end. Think about old cassette tapes. To get to the next song, the current song needs to be either played all the way through or fast forwarded through; this kind of memory is called **sequential memory**. RAM is more like a CD. To get the next song, just hit next.

Remember, the main memory temporarily holds the information while the CPU processes it. As a result, the more RAM a computer has, the less it needs to retrieve information and the faster it can run programs (as well as multiple programs simultaneously).

Peripherals

Most everything else in the computer is called a **peripheral**, which means they operate at the outside edge of the computers. These peripherals— not the CPU and main memory— are how the user interacts with the computer. The peripherals include all the I/O devices and the secondary memory.

Secondary Memory

The **secondary memory** is all other memory outside of the main memory that the computer accesses. Secondary memory is used for long term storage and gets physically changed when files are saved or deleted. Because of this change it is slower than main memory (although still very fast). The secondary memory is much larger than the main memory and usually only gets changed when a user changes the information, such as saving or deleting. Common secondary memory devices are the hard drive, floppy disks, CD-ROMs, USB storage devices, and flash drives. These things hold the software (OS and Apps) that the main memory will access.

I/O Devices

The **input and output (I/O) devices** are how the user interacts with the computer. Without these devices, the computer would not be very helpful. The most common input devices are the keyboard and the mouse— they tell the computer when something is typed in or something is clicked. Other devices that take input are joysticks, microphones, and scanners. Output devices take something from the computer and send it to the user. The most common output devices are the monitor and the printer—others include speakers and virtual reality goggles. In some cases, a device can be both input and output devices. An example of such a device is a touch screen monitor as it takes input when touched and displays output as a monitor.

Volatile vs. Nonvolatile

Another difference between main and secondary memory is that main memory is usually volatile and secondary is usually nonvolatile. This difference refers to the stored information and the power supply. **Volatile** means that information is deleted when the power is turned off whereas in the case of **nonvolatile** the information remains. For example, when a computer is shut down, all the main memory is wiped clean, but thankfully the secondary memory will remain as is!

As mentioned earlier, the computer only reads 0's and 1's at its lowest level. A good way to think of this is by considering the computer like a light switch—it is either on or off. In terms of RAM, the computer can just mark the 'switch' on or off, but a floppy disk and a CD-ROM are a little different. Floppy disks are magnetic, and CD's and DVD's use light. The way a CD works is that there is a smooth surface and pits; the pits represent a 1 and the smooth part a

0. CD-R's and CD-RW's differ in that they have a surface that when heated to one temperature is reflective and non-reflective when heated to another.

The Power of 2

In everyday use, we use a number system that uses numbers from 0-9. So, every number we use has ten different options in each place. As in decagon or decathlon, the prefix *dec-* means ten; so, it makes sense that our number system starts with *dec-*. The number system we use daily is called base 10 or **decimal** and it uses 10 numbers ranging from zero to nine or **digits**. In base 2 or **binary** there are only two numbers used, zero and one. So, just like in the words bicycle, bifocal, or bipartisan, the prefix *bi-* means two. Each number in binary is called a **bit**, which is very small. These bits are so small that it is more practical to talk about them in bunches of eight, otherwise known as a **byte**.

Each address in memory contains one byte of information, but most information is larger than one byte, so multiple addresses are used when storing them. One byte is considered small today, so instead of talking about them in the millions, use the larger units below. Since the computer only uses 0's and 1's, everything is measured in base two, which will be defined in the section concerning binary numbers. So, one byte is 2 to the 0th power or one. The next unit is the kilobyte, which is 2 to the 10th power or 1,024. Notice that it is more than 1000 bytes, which most consider a kilo. A megabyte is 2^{20}, a gigabyte 2^{30}, and a terabyte 2^{40}.

Unit	Actual # of bytes (exponent)	Actual # of bytes (decimal form)	Approximate # of bytes
byte	2^0	1	One
kilobyte	2^{10}	1,024	One Thousand
megabyte	2^{20}	1,048,576	One Million
gigabyte	2^{30}	1,073,741,824	One Billion
terabyte	2^{40}	1,099,511,627,776	One Trillion

Sometimes when companies release hardware, such as hard drives or smart phones, they will consider a megabyte as one million bytes instead of 2^{20} bytes or a gigabyte as one billion bytes instead of 2^{30} bytes. If an mp3 player is 20 GB, the company will only put 20 billion bytes of memory in it, when 20 GB should have more than 21.4 75 billion bytes. In this case, the user is tricked and really has fewer than 19 GB of storage.

Converting Binary to Decimal Format

Understanding the base 10, or decimal system, will make understanding the base 2, or binary system, easier. Binary works in the same exact way as decimal, except that the digits range from 0 to 1; instead of using powers of 10, therefore, binary uses powers of two. For example, the first digit is multiplied by 2^0, not 10^0, the second digit is multiplied by 2^1, not 10^1, and so forth. The places in the decimal system go 1, 10, 100, 1000... from right to left, and in binary, they go 1, 2, 4, 8, 16, 32, 64.... Here is an example of a binary number: 1101 0010

Binary → Decimal

To convert from binary to decimal, simply add the values in binary that are "on" (1 represents on and 0 represents off).

$\underline{1}$ $\underline{0}$ $\underline{0}$ $\underline{1}$ = 8 + 1 = 9
8 4 2 1

$\underline{1}$ $\underline{1}$ $\underline{1}$ $\underline{1}$ = 8 + 4 + 2 + 1 = 15
8 4 2 1

$\underline{0}$ $\underline{1}$ $\underline{0}$ $\underline{1}$ $\underline{1}$ $\underline{1}$ $\underline{0}$ $\underline{0}$ = 64+16+8+4 = 92
128 64 32 16 8 4 2 1

Decimal → Binary

To convert decimal to binary, simply figure out (from left to right) if the binary value needs to be "on" (or a 1). If turning the value on does not make the sum of the number exceed the number, then it should be a "1" (otherwise it is a 0).

23 → 1 0 1 1 1 → *16 is on since it is less than 23,*
     16 8 4 2 1   *8 is off since 16 + 8 is greater than 23*

46 → 1   0 1 1 1 0 → *32 is on since it is less than 46,*
     32 16 8 4 2 1 *16 is off since 32 + 16 is greater than 46*

101→ 1   1   0 0 1 0 1 → *64 is on since it is less than 101,*
     64 32 16 8 4 2 1 *32 is on since 64+32 is less than 101*

Hexadecimal

Hexadecimal (also known as **base 16**) is a common number system in computer science. Since there are only 10 single digits (0-9), the first six letters are used to represent the remaining 6 characters (a-f). Each character in hexadecimal represents 4 bits (or a half of a byte). To represent a full byte, two hexadecimal characters are used. These are from **00** (representing 0) to **ff** (representing 255). The chart on the following page shows what each hexadecimal digit represents:

Decimal	Hexadecimal	Binary
0	0	0000 0000
1	1	0000 0001
2	2	0000 0010
3	3	0000 0011
4	4	0000 0100
5	5	0000 0101
6	6	0000 0110
7	7	0000 0111
8	8	0000 1000
9	9	0000 1001
10	a	0000 1010
11	b	0000 1011
12	c	0000 1100
13	d	0000 1101
14	e	0000 1110
15	f	0000 1111

When a hexadecimal number is larger than a **nybble** (or half of a byte), the left most hex digit is worth more, just like in any other base. In the decimal number 123, the 3 is worth 3 since it is in the ones place, but the 1 is worth 100 since it is in the one-hundreds place.

Hexadecimal → Binary

To convert a hexadecimal number into binary, look at each nybble individually:

```
d3b → d = 1101, 3 = 0011, b = 1011 → 1101 0011
1011
40f → 4 = 0100, 0 = 0000, f = 1111 → 0100 0000
1111
```

To convert these to decimal, just follow the steps to convert binary to decimal from earlier in this unit.

Binary → Hexadecimal

To convert for binary to hexadecimal, just follow the reverse of above:

```
1001 1100 0001 → 1001 = 9, 1100 = c, 0001 = 1 →
9c1
0110 0011 1110 → 0110 = 6, 0011 = 3, 1110 = e →
63e
```

The reason our society uses base ten is because that is the numbers of fingers we have, making early counting simple. This is easy because it is what we know, but it is debated that **base 8** or **octal** would be the easiest to use, especially in computing. Since base 10 uses numbers 0-9, base 8 would use 0-7 (there would be no 8 or 9). These numbers could be 8 symbols or emoji's, if everyone agreed on a standard. For this example, let's stick to 0-7. The ones place (10^0) would still be the ones place (8^0), but the 10 (10^1) would be the eights places (8^1). Every place after that would increase by a power of 8 instead of by a power of 10 (or a power of 2 in the case of binary and a power of 16 in the case of hexadecimal).

Base 8 → Decimal

Converting base 8 is just like converting binary, but instead of the places doubling, they increase by a power of 8:

```
174 →  1   7 4  →  1*64 + 7*8 + 4*1 = 64+56+4 = 114
      64  8 1

520 →  5   2 0  →  5*64 + 2*8 + 0*1 = 64+16+0 = 336
      64  8 1
```

ASCII

ASCII stands for American Standard Code for Information Interchange. Since computes can only understand numbers, letters and symbols must be converted into numbers. This includes lowercase letters, uppercase letters, symbols, spaces, tabs, delete, backspace, and more. The first 32 characters (0-31) were used for teletype machines and are now considered obsolete.

Important Vocabulary

- **Applications** – includes word processors, photo editing software, web browsers, games, music programs, almost everything else on the computer excluding saved files
- **ASCII** – American Standard Code for Information Interchange
- **Binary** – base 2, number system that uses 0, 1
- **Bit** – each number in the binary system, 0 or 1
- **Byte** – 8 bits
- **Central Processing Unit (CPU)** – carries out every command or process on the computer and can be thought of as the brain of the computer
- **Computer** – an electronic device that processes data according to a set of instructions or commands, known as a program
- **Core** – the central processing unit (CPU) and the main memory
- **Decimal** – base 10, number system that used 0-9
- **Digit** – each number in the decimal system, 0-9

- **Hardware** – the physical parts of the computer. Devices such as the monitor, keyboard, speakers, wires, chips, cables, plugs, disks, printers, mice, and many other

- **Hexadecimal** – base 16, number system that uses 0-9 and a-f

- **Input and output (I/O) devices** – how the user interacts with the computer

- **Main memory** – memory that temporarily stores information while it is being sent to the CPU, also called RAM

- **Nonvolatile** – does not need a power supply, information is physically written to the device

- **Nybble (or Nibble)** – half of a byte, 4 bits

- **Operating System** – the visual representation of the computer

- **Peripherals** – the input and output (I/O) devices and the secondary memory

- **Random Access Memory** – memory that can be retrieved or written to anywhere without having to go through all the previous memory

- **Secondary memory** – used for long term storage and gets physically changed when files are saved or deleted

- **Sequential Memory** – memory used to store back-up data on a tape

- **Software** – a series of ones and zeros at the lowest level and cannot physically be touched and is usually stored on the hard drive of the computer and includes the operating system and the applications.
- **Volatile** – needs a power supply, information is deleted when the power is turned off

Suggested Reading

- "Digital Explosion." *Blown to Bits*. Chapter 1. Pages 1-17
- "Introduction." *Nine Algorithms that Changed the Future*. Chapter 1. Pages 7-12

Unit 2 – Photo Editing and Adobe Photoshop

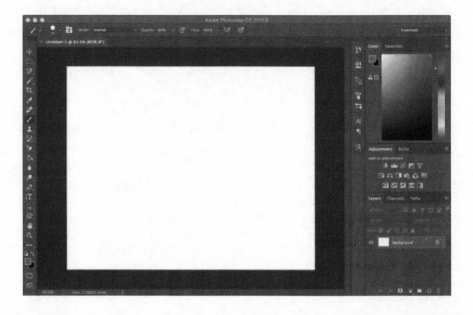

Intro to Adobe Photoshop

Adobe Photoshop is a graphics editor developed and published by Adobe Systems. This program is the current market leader for commercial bitmap and image manipulation, and in addition to Adobe Acrobat, it is one of the most well-known pieces of software produced by Adobe Systems. It is considered the industry standard in most, if not all, jobs related to the use of visual elements. It is usually referred to simply as "Photoshop."

Photoshop allows a user to create and modify digital images, or rather images in electronic form. Some of the major uses for the software include creating original artwork, modifying or combining existing pictures, adding text or special effects for a webpage, and restoring or touching up old photographs. Existing images can come from many places including images downloaded from the web, imported from a digital camera, or imported by using a scanner. Once a piece of art is created or imported, the user can now modify it. These images can be rotated or resized; text can be added; colors can be changed; and the original images can be combined with other images. To make such changes, one must modify the **pixels** or tiny dots that represent a certain color. The more pixels an image has, the better quality it will be. More pixels will also translate to larger files.

Once the image is ready to be saved, there are many choices of file types to save as. The most common are **.psd**, **.png**, **.jpg**, and **.gif**. **.psd** is the Photoshop file format, which will be larger and will not be able to be read by many other applications. The other three methods can be read by most applications and are significantly smaller in size than the Photoshop format.

When modifying images in Photoshop, chances are the user will want to save both the old and new images in case the user needs to use the image again or if they make a mistake. To make sure the old image stays intact, use the *Save as...* command as soon as the image is opened and when saving the modified image, then name the new image something different. There is now a copy of the original that will not be touched and can be opened to start from scratch.

The Workspace

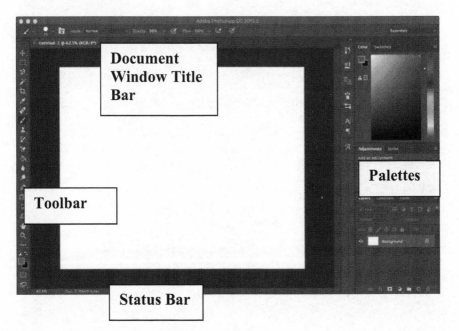

The **workspace** is the area in-between the tool option bar and the status bar. The workspace includes all the palettes, the toolbar, and the document windows being worked on.

The **title bar** contains the name of the program as well as the close, minimize, and maximize buttons.

The **tool options bar** is located under the menu bar and shows more options for the selected tool from the toolbox. When a new tool is selected, the tool option bar will change to accommodate the selected tools. This option bar contains very useful additions to the selected tool that vary from tool to tool.

The **palettes** are small windows which start stacked up on the right side of the workspace. These palettes may be moved anywhere in the workspace and reordered in anyway desired. The most useful palettes are the history palette and the layer palette. These palettes show the last twenty actions performed and information about each layer in the image respectively.

The **status bar**, located at the bottom of the screen, displays information about the file size and the active tool.

Layers

A layer is a part of the image that can be modified independently. Think of the books that show the different systems of the body. The pages are clear and can be folded back to see what the layer underneath looks like. Photoshop can support up to 8000 layers. Layers can make the file size very large, however, since all the images that are blocked by the other layers are still there. To make the file size smaller, the image can be flattened. Flattening an image discards all the image information that cannot be seen or that is blocked; saving as most other formats will automatically flatten an image since they do not support layers.

The **layer palette** shows the active layer by highlighting it and multiple layers can be selected by holding down shift or control/command. To make layers easier to see, individual layers can be hidden. To do this, click the eye icon to the left of the layer. The layer can be seen again by clicking the empty box where the eye used to be. The same effect can be achieved by changing the layer's opacity to 0% from the top of the layer palette.

The **toolbox** contains frequently used Photoshop commands. Each tool is marked by a graphical representation of what the tool does. When the user moves the pointer over a tool, a screen tip will appear stating the name of the tool and the keyboard shortcut in parenthesis. Some tools have other tools hidden behind them—this is denoted by a small triangle at the bottom right hand corner of the tool. To see the hidden tools, hold down the pointer on the tool or right click.

Move Tool	
	Marquee Tools
Lasso Tools	
	Magic Wand Tool
Crop Tool	
Healing Brush/Patch Tool	
	Paint Brush/ Pencil
Clone Tool	
	Eraser Tools
Paint Bucket/Gradient Tools	
	Blur/Sharpen/Smudge
Dodge/Burn/Sponge Tools	
	Pen Tool
Type Tools	
Hand Tool	
	Zoom Tool
Set Background/Foreground Colors	

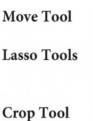

Tools

Selecting

When editing or combining images, it might be useful to take one piece of the image and either move it to another image or edit it. There are many ways to select parts of images. A marquee tool can be used, whether rectangular or elliptical.

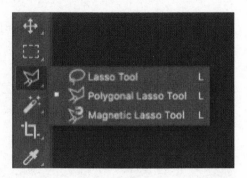

One of the three lasso tools can be also used—these include regular, polygonal, or magnetic. The magic wand can be used if the background is significantly different from the image.

The **marquee tool** should be used when the object is either a rectangular or round shape. The **magic wand** automatically detects changes in color, so if the object is on a solid colored background, this would be useful. The best way to get all other irregular shapes is to use the lasso tools. When tracing the whole image by hand, the **regular lasso** tool should be used. The **polygonal lasso** is useful when the object has all straight edges. The **magnetic lasso** automatically detects changes in color like the magic wand tool. With this tool, trace the object roughly, and the lasso will set anchors along the edges of the image.

For each of these tools in the tool option bar, there are three useful options for selections. These options include the **New Selection, Add to Selection,** and **Subtract from Selection** illustrated in the first three options after the lasso above. The new selection tool is used when starting from scratch, the add to selection tool is used when a part was missing from the original selection or another object needs to be added, and the subtract from selection tool is used when part of the selection does not need to be included in the object.

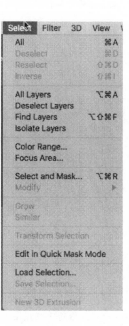

There are also useful options in the *Select* menu under the menu bar—these include the *All, Deselect,* and *Inverse* options. All selects the whole layer, deselect gets rid of any selections on the page, and inverse makes anything selected, unselected and anything unselected, selected. There are also useful options under the same menu and the *Modify* option. Here the selection can be expanded or contracted.

Once an object is selected, use the **move tool** to drag the selection from one image to another or to move it within the same image. If the move tool is not selected, then dragging the selection will only move the marquee or the dotted line, not the image selection itself. Right clicking inside the selection also allows for a new layer to be created from the selection, either by copying or cutting the selection.

Layer Masks

Another way to select something in an image is to erase everything else around it. The problem with this is that once it is erased, it can be hard to get back if an error is made. To solve

this problem, masks can be used. Masks are a way of cropping out parts of pictures without modifying the pixels, so if there is a mistake it can easily be corrected by changing the mask and not the picture

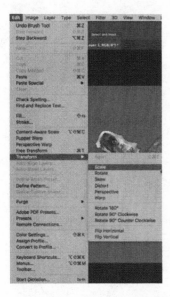

itself. If a layer is locked as a background, double the click the layer in the layer palette, name it, and click ok to create a new layer from it. To begin masking click the mask button that looks like a square with a circle cut out at the bottom of the layer palette. This can also be done by going to the Layer menu and selecting Layer Mask and reveal all. Once a mask is on the layer, then the effect of erasing can be achieved by painting the mask black. Alternatively, the mask can give the opposite effect by painting it white. It is important to make sure the paint brush being use is set to 100% hardness to have a perfect edge; without this the picture will appear to have a glowing edge. While using masks, use the zoom tool to get closer to the pixel level to get a crisp edge. By holding down shift and clicking with the paint brush, the dots will connect in a straight line, also making the edges much crisper. A list of useful shortcuts can be found at the end of this unit.

Master Copy

Once an image has been masked, it is a good idea to duplicate this layer and lock the original as a master copy. If mistakes are made that cannot be change, then a new duplicate can be made from that master copy. One way to create a duplicate of what is masked is to hold Ctrl down and click on the thumbnail of the mask; this selects the white area of the mask. Next, make sure the thumbnail of the image is selected and select Layer… New… Layer via copy from the menu bar. Double click the name of the original copy, rename it Master, and the click the padlock icon at the top of the layer palette. Now that the master copy is locked, turn the layer's visibility off and drag it to the bottom of the layer palette.

Transforming

Transformations are a way to scale, skew, distort, warp, flip, rotate, and perspective a layer. The most useful of these is scale. Scaling up is usually not a great idea, since the layer might become pixilated. To scale down a layer select Edit... Transform... Scale or use the short cut for free transform: Ctrl/Command +T. To ensure that the dimensions of the layer do not get distorted, hold down shift and grab the layer by a corner. When transformations are complete, press enter to accept the changes or esc to cancel the transformation.

Filters

Filters are the way to edit the pixels in the image to give it a desired look or feel. There are several filters built-in to Photoshop. The downside of filters is that it does change the pixels, so the only way to remove a filter is to undo or step backwards, but by applying a smart filter to a layer, the information in the original layer will be stored and filters can be removed or changed easily. If the file has been saved and closed, then there is no

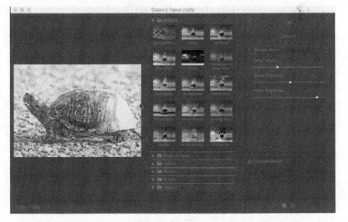

way to get back to the original image if a smart filter was not applied. Some categories of filters include **Artistic Filters, Stylize Filters, Render Filters, Noise Filters, Blur Filters,** and **Sketch Filters.** All the filters can be seen by selecting the *Filter* menu in the menu bar. Under each category of filter, there are many actual filters such as **Colored Pencil, Smudge Stick, Watercolor, Pinch, Ripple, Wave, Gaussian Blur, Tiles, Clouds,** and **Glowing Edges.** Most of these filters have sub-menus as well that are indicated with an ellipsis. To see most of the categories at the same time select *Filter Gallery....*

Layer Styles

Layer styles are a good way to add effects to a layer. Unlike filters, layer styles can be turned on or off and changes as needed, even if the file has been saved and closed. Most of the options in layer styles affect the edge of the layer, so if a layer takes up the whole canvas, then layer styles might not work the best. A few useful styles are the drop shadow, outer glow, bevel and emboss, and stroke. To bring up the layer styles window, double click to the right of the layer name on the layer palette or select *Layer... Layer Styles* from the menu bar. The check boxes can turn the styles on and off and more options can be seen by clicking on the actual name of the style.

Gradients

A gradient is a fill consisting of two or more colors blending together. The default gradient colors will be the current foreground and background, but these can be changed to infinite possibilities by clicking on the preview of the gradient in the tool option bar. Gradients can also use transparency to achieve certain effects. In addition to colors, there are also five different types of gradients: linear, radial, angle, reflected and diamond.

Type

By using the Type Tool, text can be added to Photoshop to help get a message across to an audience. Example of this are magazine and newspaper advertisements. Many different fonts and colors are used to emphasize certain parts of the overall image in such advertisements. Text or type should be used sparingly in Photoshop as most the overall file should be the image itself. Type reinforces or complements the existing image. The type should be very direct and large enough to be seen easily. The type should not be so large that it takes away from the image, however.

Font Families

There are three main font families: **serif, sans serif,** and **symbols.**
The word *sans* translates to "without," and a *serif* is a tail, or stoke, at
the end of a character. In other words, serif fonts contain a tail or
stroke on most characters and sans serif does not. Symbols are
unique characters such as $, #, &, @, and *.

Editing Fonts

When the type tool is used, it
automatically adds a new
layer to the file. Simply click
and type to add text. To
change the size, color, or
font of the text, highlight the
text and change these things
in the tool option bar at the
top of the window. Selecting

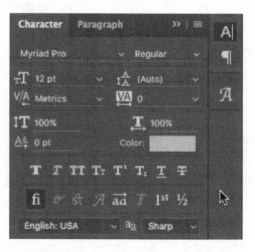

all the text in a layer can be done by double clicking on the
thumbnail of the text layer in the layer palette. For more option to
adjust the font, such as tracking or kerning, use the character palette
which looks like an A with a vertical bar to the right when collapsed.
Many characteristics of the fonts can be changed. One aspect that
can be modified is the type spacing or the space in-between each
character. The type spacing can be set to monotype spacing or
proportional spacing. Monotype makes every character take up the

same amount of space (i would take up the same amount of space as w). Proportional takes up a different amount of space depending on the letter (this book uses proportional spacing!).

Shortcuts

Ctrl + N:	New document
Ctrl + O:	Open document
Ctrl + S:	Save
Ctrl + A:	Select All
Ctrl + D:	Deselect
Ctrl + Z:	Undo
Ctrl + Alt + Z:	Step Backwards (Undo more than 1 step)
Ctrl + Shift + Z:	Step Forward (Redo more than one step)
Alt + Mouse Scroll:	Zoom in/out
Space Bar:	Hand tool (move around zoomed picture)
V:	Move tool
B:	Brush tool
G:	Paint Bucket/Gradient Tool
E:	Eraser
T:	Type Tool
M:	Marquee tools (rectangular, elliptical)
L:	Lasso tools (free lasso, polygonal, magnetic)
W:	Magic wand tool
D:	Set foreground/background to black/white
X:	Flip foreground and background color

[:   Make brush one size smaller
] :   Make brush one size larger
Shift + click: Paint/draw straight lines
Ctrl + J: New layer via copy
Ctrl + Click (on layer thumbnail):   Select contents of the layer
(white part of masks)

Unit 3 – Spreadsheets and Microsoft Excel

Intro to Microsoft Excel

Microsoft Excel is a spreadsheet program written and distributed by Microsoft for computers using the Microsoft Windows and Mac OS operating systems. The program features an intuitive interface and graphing tools and is capable of a high level of calculation, which along with aggressive marketing has made Excel one of the most popular computer applications to date. This program is the overwhelmingly dominant spreadsheet application available for these platforms and has been so since version 5 in 1993 and its bundling as part of Microsoft Office.

A spreadsheet is basically a grid used to store information (usually numbers) that consists of rows and columns. **Rows** go from left to right like rows of seats in a movie theater and are labeled using numbers starting at 1 in Excel, there are over one million possible rows. **Columns** go from top to bottom like the columns that used to hold up Greek ruins—these are labeled using letters starting with A. When more than 26 columns are used, double letters are used continuing with AA, AB, AC, AD, etc. then triple letters starting with AAA, AAB… all the way until XFD.

Each individual piece of the grid, or where the rows and columns intersect, are called **cells**. Cells are named by using the column letter and then the row number; A1 is the cell at the top left of the spreadsheet. Three basic items can be placed into the cells: labels, constants, and formulas. A **label** is the text that describes some part of the spreadsheet, such as name or amount. Labels are not for the computer but rather for the human to better understand what the information in the cell is talking about. A **constant** is any number that the user puts into the spreadsheet; this will not change unless the user changes it manually. A **formula** is a math equation that can perform math on existing cells; all formulas must start with an equals sign. Some examples of formulas are *=5 + 6*5, =2*F4 – A7*. Notice that F4 and A7 are cells, so whatever number is in that cell will be what is subtracted or multiplied. If there is a constant or nothing in that cell, errors may occur.

Functions

Excel has many built-in functions that can help manipulate data. Some of these functions include finding minimums, maximums, averages, sums, trig functions, conditional statements, and many more. There are more than 200 functions in Excel. These can be found by either knowing the name of the function or by going to *Formulas...Insert Function...* A list of functions will then pop-up that can be narrowed down by searching or selecting a category. Notice that all functions (like formulas) begin with an equals sign.

At the bottom of the window, there will be a brief description on what the

Formula Builder

Q Search

Most Recently Used
MAX
SUM
COUNTIF
IF
DATE
MIN
AVERAGE
COUNT
SIN
SUMIF
All
ABS

Insert Function

fx **MAX**

Returns the largest value in a set of values. Ignores logical values and text.

Syntax

MAX(number1,number2,...)

- **number1**: number1,number2,... are 1 to 255 numbers, empty cells, logical values, or text

More help on this function

function does. A more detailed description will be given when the function is selected.

The following chart shows some useful functions and how they look when entered into the cell:

Name	Description	Sample Code	Appears in Cell
AVG	Finds the average from a list of numbers	=AVG(A1, A4, A6, A8)	4.75
MIN & MAX	Finds the minimum/maximum value of a list of numbers and returns that number	=MIN(D1:D9) = MAX(B13:B23)	37 104
COUNT & COUNTA	Counts how many cells have numerical data. CountA counts all data, text included	=COUNT(A1:K30) =COUNTA(A1:K30)	29 46
SUM	Adds up all the values and returns the answer	=SUM(A1,A5,B3,D5)	73

IF	This can return different things depending if the condition is met. The first thing after the condition is if it is true and the second if false	=IF(B1<C1,"You win", "You lose")	You lose

Embedding Functions

Functions and formulas can sometimes work together and some function can even be embedded, or inserted, into other functions. For example, if you wanted to find what group of cells had the highest average, then you might write it like this:

=min(average(A1:A20), average(B1:B20), average(C1:C20))

Formatting

Formatting is a way to make the data in the spreadsheet more visually appealing. This can be done by changing the look of numbers, the font, color, size, adding borders, or aligning the text in different ways. By right clicking on a cell, or selecting *Formatting... format cells...* under the

Home tab, the Format Cells window will appear. There will be six tabs to choose from at the top of this window. These tabs can be easily mastered by experimenting with each of the different options.

Conditional Formatting

Excel has some built-in formatting tools that will automatically do calculation for the user. Some of these include highlighting cells that meet specific criteria; such as equaling a value, being greater than a certain value, or being less than a certain value. There are also ones that can highlight cells that are in the top or bottom 5 or 10 or any given value; this can also be done with percentages. Conditional formatting also can turn the cells into mini graphs using data bars or different color schemes. These are determined by the highest and lowest values and can be modified by going into more options.

To clear conditional formatting, highlight the cells and select *clear rules* in the conditional formatting menu.

Auto Formatting

Instead of trying to add colors and borders to the spreadsheet by hand, there are several pre-made templates that can change the look of the data. To use one of these, select the cells that are to be formatted, then select *Formatting... Format as Table...* from the **Home** menu bar.

Charts

Excel can also create charts and graphs from the data in the spreadsheet. There are several different charts that can be created, the most common being the bar, pie, and line charts. Under each chart type, there are sub-types that can give the graph more effects, such as

making it three-dimensional or other effects which show relationships throughout the data. Remember that a line graph shows change in data over time. To choose the type of chart desired select the desired chart type under the **Insert** tab.

 Before a chart type is selected, the data range needs to be chosen. This can be done by highlighting the cells that contain the data. To select cells that are not connected, choose the first set of cells, then hold down the Ctrl key and select the next set. Once the data is selected, click on the type of chart as shown in the picture above.

Titles can be added as well as  axes names, legends, and data labels using the **Design, Layout, and Format** tabs that will appear in the tabs when the chart is clicked on. Some of these tabs are shown below.

Printing

There are many options when it comes to printing an Excel document. These options can all be found under *File... Page Setup...*

Under the Page tab, the orientation of the page can be set (either vertical or horizontal). The page may also be scaled to fit a desired number of pages. Another useful tab here is the *Sheet tab*. The most useful item under the *Sheet tab* is the Gridlines checkbox under the Print section. This tab will show the lines in the spreadsheet when checked. Excel will not show the gridlines by default

Unit 4 – Data and Compression

Why Compress Data?

In today's world there is endless audio, images, videos, apps, and more being saved, sent, or downloaded than ever before. Even though sizes of hard drives are increasing, uncompressed files will fill them up quickly. For example, an uncompressed, 90 minute, HD (1080p) movie would take up approximately 1 terabyte of hard drive space. Using a common compression format for video called H.264 could store the same 90-minute movie in 1080p using only 65 gigabytes, 15 times smaller than the uncompressed version. By using a video space calculator, it is easy to see how different formats (or amount to frames per second) can dramatically change file size.

This is just referring to space on a personal hard drive. Today, most of this digital information is sent over the Internet (more on that in Unit 5). This means, the larger the file size, the longer it takes to download. Or even worse, the image quality and buffering of streaming movies or TV shows! With the amount of data be sent over the internet every second, it is important to keep file sizes small without compromising the quality of the material.

Heuristic Approach

In programming, a **heuristic approach** is an approach that gives results that are "good enough" when an exact answer is not necessary. This is seen in the famous Travelling Salesman problem, which tries to map out the shortest distance between many cities. This problem is simple with a few cities, but gets exponentially more difficult as more cities are added. This problem is **computationally hard**, meaning even a computer would take too long to find the exact solution. An instance using 85,900 "cities" was solved in 2006, but took the equivalent of a computer running 24 hours a day for 136 years. The amount of time and computation power to find this outweighed to result. It would have been better to find a "good" route in a much shorter amount of time.

A heuristic approach is also appropriate when compressing data. The "good enough" solution in compression will be the relationship between size and quality. To keep text, images, audio, video, etc. from losing any quality, the size of the compressed file will not be much smaller than the original. In the case of compressing a song (like turning it into an mp3), a heuristic approach would be to take out enough of the data, but still make the song sound high quality on a personal speaker.

Lossy vs. Lossless

When compressing data, a heuristic approach may be the right choice. If a smaller size is more important than quality, it is okay to lose some data. Losing data during compression is known as **lossy** compression. Most of the time this loss of data cannot be detected by the human eye or ear. If a red color was changed slightly, the human eye would not be able to see the difference. So, when an image is compressed, the computer may look at colors that are very similar and change them all to the same color. When there are millions of colors, this could save a lot of file size and make the file load faster on websites and send faster through email. For an audio file, this might mean that the **sample rate** or **bits per second** is reduced. The audio file could be reduced from 96 kHz to 44.1 kHz without noticing a big enough difference to justify the much larger file size.

Other times it is important to get the exact solution, meaning that when a file is uncompressed, it need to have all the original information that it had before it was compressed. When compressing text files or emails, it is important to maintain all the original information; otherwise, certain letter or words might be missing. This kind of compression is known as **lossless** compression, it does not lose any data during compression.

Metadata

Most of the time, the data itself is not enough and additional information about the data is needed. This "data about the data" is known as **metadata** and even though the Greek prefix means "after", it usually comes at the very beginning of the file. Most file types require metadata and have a strict set of rules of where it is located and how long it needs to be. Some of this metadata could include title, author, keywords, date created, location it was created, file size, height, width, and many more. Examples of what this metadata might look like will be discussed later in this chapter.

Text Compression

Large file sizes might not seem like a big deal, but as we will see in Unit 5, smaller file sizes are critical when sending information thousands of miles in the matter of seconds over the Internet. Images, audio files and videos are much relatively much larger than text files, but with the amount of emails and text messages sent every day, text compression is just as important. It is also important that no data is lost when text is compresses. Losing 10% of an email might make it unreadable. So, text compression will always be **lossless**. An easy way to think about text compression is by looking at common words or patterns of letters and representing them with a single character or letter. Let's assume that every time the word "and" appeared in this book, it was replaced with a plus sign. "and" appears approximately 535 in this book, that is 1605 characters. If it was replaced with a plus sign, it would only take up 535 characters. What if it was expanded to "_and_" with one space before and after the word? That represents 2675 characters that, using a plus sign, would only take 535 characters (plus 6 characters of metadata to tell the next user that the file was compressed). Imaging if more common words or common letter grouping were changed into symbols. The letters "th" appear almost 3000 times in this book. With just swapping "and" and "th", it reduces the length of this book by almost 6000 characters, that is over 4 full pages! This would all be useless if the **metadata** explaining what words or letter groups were swapped.

Compressing Text Example

♣	wood
♦	chuck
♥	♣♦
♠	could

How much ♣ ♠a ♥♦if a ♥♠♦♣?

By following the key (or metadata) to the left, the message can be uncompressed to read:

How much wood could a woodchuck chuck if a woodchuck could chuck wood?

The original message contains 58 characters and the compressed message contains 20 characters in the message and 20 characters in the key (metadata). This doesn't seem like much, but this simple compression made the file about 30% smaller. Imagine taking that uncompressed HD movie from the beginning of this chapter and making it 30% smaller. The original file was a terabyte, so this would save about 300 gigabytes. Obviously, video cannot be compressed this way, but there are even more ways to compress video that makes it much smaller than the original. But think of how much text is on a computer: word documents, emails, and more. If everyone tried sending dozens of uncompressed emails every day, then internet speeds would be at risk. This will be discussed in the next Unit.

Image Compression

A **pixel**, short for picture element, is the basic unit of color on a computer display. The size of pixels on a screen can change depending on the resolution of the display. To have a larger number of pixels on a display, they size of the pixel must be smaller; this will result in a better-quality image. When picture is scanned into the computer or a digital photo is taken, the image must be turned into millions of pixels. These pixels can be represented as binary numbers, so the computer can understand them. When pixels are too large the image looks blocky, this is called **pixelation**. Contrary to what is seen in movies, there is no way to "enhance" these images, since they do not contain the binary information for the missing pixels.

Black and White Images

Looking at a simple example of converting binary code to a black and white image will help clarify how 1's and 0's can display an image on a monitor. Black and white work well for this example, since they can be represented by a single bit. 0 = black, 1 = white. In addition to the color data, there also must be metadata to know such things as the height and the width.

00000110 0000101 10101010 10101110 10101010 10101000

width   height   pixel data

metadata

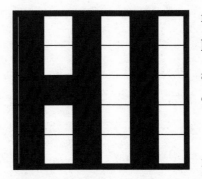

In this example, the two bytes (16 bits) represents the width one byte for each. information is predetermined by the metadata is long and and height, This kind of file type and every file of that type must follow the same rules. If the first byte is converted into binary, it equals 6, the height is 5. So, this image is 6 pixels by 5 pixels. The remaining 4 bytes of this file would represent the pixel color, black or white. Just like reading, start at the top left and fill in "1's" will black and continue to the next row when needed. The result will say "Hi".

Color Images and RGB Values

There are two main color models to consider: CMYK and RGB. **CMYK** is used for printing and stands for **C**yan, **M**agenta, **Y**ellow, and Black (**K**ey) where the number associated with each letter is the percent of each color used. This color model is a subtractive model, meaning white is the color of the paper and black is the combination of all the colors. Black is usually a separate ink cartridge in printers, since it is more cost effective than combining all three of the other colors and replace them more often.

RGB (which stands for **R**ed, **G**reen, and **B**lue) refers to the color of light used in most monitors or screens and is an additive color model. This means that no light is black and the combination of all light is white. Instead of using a percent from 0-100, RGB uses one byte (2^8 or 0-255) to represent each color. Since there are three colors, each RGB value (1 pixel) is 3 bytes of data (24 bits), much larger than the 1 bit a black and white image uses. If the RGB value of a color was (255, 0, 0), all the red light is on and no green or blue light is on, so it would be a red light. Likewise, (0, 0, 255) would be blue. Using 24 bits to represents color gives 2^{24} possible combinations, that is 16,777,216 colors.

One way that color images can be compressed is by looking at colors that are very similar to one another. When there are almost 17 million colors, a color only a few bits away from another will look identical to the human eye. So, compression algorithms for images take these similar colors and just save them all as the same color, most of the time without changing the quality of the image. But, when these algorithms are too aggressive, color banding occurs like in the image below.

Important Vocabulary

- **Computationally hard** – a problem that even a computer would take too long to find the exact solution

- **Heuristic approach** – an approach that gives results that are "good enough" when an exact answer is not necessary.

- **Lossless** – a data compression that does not lose data during compression

- **Lossy** – a data compression that loses data during compression

- **Bit Rate** – the number of bits that can be processed per second

- **Sample rate** – usually measured in bits per second, how often an analog signal is used when converting to digital

- **Metadata** – additional data about the main data, usually at the beginning of a file

- **Pixelation** – when individual pixels are too large and the image begins to look blocky

- **CMYK** – used for printing and stands for **C**yan, **M**agenta, **Y**ellow, and **B**lack (**K**ey) where the number associated with each letter is the percent of each color used

- **RGB** – stands for **R**ed, **G**reen, and **B**lue and refers to the color of light used in most monitors or screens

Suggested Reading

- "Naked in the Sunlight." *Blown to Bits.* Chapter 2. Pages 19-72

- "Ghosts in the Machine." *Blown to Bits.* Chapter 3. Pages 73-108

- "Data Compression." *Nine Algorithms that Changed the Future.* Chapter 7. Pages 78-89

Unit 5 – The Internet

Origins

A computer **network** is a group of computers that are connected so they can share resources using a data link, usually a cable or wirelessly. These networks could be a set of 20 school computers, a large business with thousands of computers that are all sharing files, or even a family with 3 computers all connecting to the same media server in their house. The **Internet** is a network of these smaller networks connected using a specific set of rules that computers use to communicate with each other. These rules are called **protocols** and the one the Internet uses is aptly named **Internet Protocol** (**IP**), which works closely with Transmission Control Protocol (**TCP**).

The Internet seems like a new thing, but it's origins date to 1969 and the Advanced Research Projects Agency Network (**ARPANET**). This was the first network to use TCP/IP protocols that are still used today (but was not the standard until 1982). The ARPANET also broke the data up into smaller, more manageable pieces called **packets** which is the basis for data communication today. Even though it was decommissioned on February 28th, 1990, the ARPANET is still considered to be the foundation of today's Internet.

IP Addresses

Just like every business and home has a unique address so the post office can deliver mail, so does every computer and device. Theses address are known as Internet Protocol Address or **IP Addresses** for short. Even though everything is stored in binary on the computer, IP Addresses are usually written so humans can understand them, like telephone numbers. Since every computer, printer, router, smart phone, and more devices are connected to the Internet, the number of IP Addresses are growing fast. These are all managed by a non-profit corporation named the Internet Assigned Number Authority (**IANA**), which is a department of Internet Corporation for Assigned Names and Numbers (**ICANN**).

IPv4 vs. IPv6

Internet Protocol has gone through many versions, but the forth version of IP routes the most Internet traffic. IPv4 uses 32-bit addresses, which gives a possible 2^{32} or 4,294,967,296 possible addresses. These addresses were broken down into 4 bytes, each separated by a period and displayed in decimal, giving a value from 0-255. An IPv4 address could look something like: **192.168.1.1**.

Four billion IP addresses seemed like more than enough back in the early 1980's when IPv4 was created, but with so many people on the Internet using multiple devices today, they have run out. In the late

1990's the Internet Engineering Task Force (**IETF**) came up with an addressing system that used 128-bits called IPv6. This gives 2^{128} possible addresses, that is more than 3.4×10^{38} possibilities. This is an extremely large number, much larger than the number of grains of sand or even number of atoms on the planet. There will never be close to that many addresses. Since writing these addresses in bits require 128 1's and 0's, they are written in hexadecimal and might look like this: **2001:0db8:85a3:0000:0000:8a2e:0370:7334**. Since there are so many unused bytes, zeros can be omitted and replaced with a double colon: **2001:0db8:85a3::8a2e:0370:7334**. Most sites have both an IPv4 and IPv6 address to prepare for a smooth transition to using only IPv6, something that most people won't even realize happened.

The Web

The Internet is commonly referred to as the World Wide Web or simply the **web**. Although the web is part of the Internet, they are not the same thing. The Internet has many services using separate protocols, the web is just one of them. Other services/protocols include e-mail (Internet Message Access Protocol or **IMAP** and Post Office Protocol or **POP**), Internet telephony (Voice over Internet or **VoIP**), and file transfer (**FTP**). The web displays websites on web browsers and uses Hypertext Transfer Protocol (**HTTP**) or Hypertext Transfer Protocol Secure (**HTTPS**) that has extra security like **SSL/TLS** (more in Unit 7). Therefore, there is always *http://* or *https://* before website names (sometime the browser hides this, but it is there).

HTML

Hyper Text Markup Language or **HTML** is the standard for creating web pages, hence the name of the protocol web pages' use: Hyper Text Transfer Protocol. A markup language is just a way to make text standout, like changing colors, fonts, alignment, etc. It is not a programming language. HTML uses tags that are between angle brackets (< and >) and is usually paired with Cascading Style Sheets (**CSS**) and **JavaScript**. More on HTML and CSS in Unit 6 and JavaScript in Unit 8.

Addressing

A website is just a file stored on a computer, also called a **server**. A server could be a home computer, part of a large server farm, or anything in-between. When a computer request a specific file (like a website) or a service from a server, it is known as the **client**. The Internet runs on this **client-server model**. A client sends a request to the server and then the server sends the requested information back to the client. The client can request the server by using its unique IP address (IPv4 or IPv6). It would be very tedious to memorize every IP address of every webpage, so instead, domain names are used.

A **domain name** is simply a name given or linked to an IP address. These are the website names that are typed into the web browser, like *www.google.com* or *wordpress.org*. Google's IP address is 8.8.8.8 (not that hard to remember) and WordPress uses 74.200.243.254 (among others). Most website also contain many pages or files besides just the home page. These files and folders use a Uniform Resource Locator or **URL** to call or locator specific files from the domain. An example of a URL is *https://www.mrhare.gov/classes/apcsp/textbook.pdf*, the domain name of this file is *www.mrhare.gov*. Most of the time when a domain name is used, the URL is automatically opening a file called *index.html* or *home.html*. So, the domain name *https://www.mrhare.gov* is opening the URL *https://www.mrhare.gov/index.html*. Any domain can also be preceded by a **subdomain** like https://*csprinciples.mrhare.gov* or *https://awesomeness.mrhare.gov*, still owned by *https://www.mrhare.gov*.

DNS

When a client request a file from a server, the first step is for the client to get the IP address of the domain name that the URL is located on. This process is kicked off by the Domain Name System (**DNS**). The DNS is one of the smaller networks that make up the Internet and contains many servers that act like phone books. These computers are called **name servers** and contain many IP addresses and their matching domain names. Most of these name servers are owned by Internet Service Providers (**ISPs**), such as Comcast, AT&T, Time Warner, Verizon, Cox, and others. If the first name server does not contain the requested domain's IP address, it will ask another name server for it. If that name server does not know it, it will ask another name server. This process will continue until the IP address is found and sent back through the name servers to the client.

Since there are so many IP addresses and domain names, most name servers only contain a small portion of them. But, there are 13 **Root Name Servers** that contain every single domain name and IP address in the world. Most of the root name servers are a network of computers, in-case of a failure. They are named A-M and are maintained by a handful of different companies, groups, and colleges. A few of these are Verisign, University of Maryland, U.S. Army Research Lab, and ICANN.

TCP/IP

After the IP address has been obtained, the client's request can be sent to the server by using the protocols TCP and IP, often paired together by saying **TCP/IP**. Even though these are almost always referred to together, they are two separate steps in the process. On the client side, TCP is the next step. In this step, the request is broken down in to smaller, more manageable pieces called **packets**. TCP also numbers these packets, so when they are put back together (on the client side), they will be in the correct order. When TCP finishes, the packets are handed off to IP. The IP then creates and attached addresses to each packet before it sends them off to the physical Internet to keep track of all the packets.

Fault Tolerant

Since the packets are numbered, it is easy for TCP to keep track of missing packets. If the server or host sees that packet number 25 is missing, it will request it again. Once the packet makes it to the destination, it is reassembled into the original file. This ensures that all packets eventually make it to the correct destination. The Internet is **fault tolerant** since if there is an error, the system will still work properly. Without this property, the whole system could fail if one packet was misplaced.

Routers

Once the DNS, TCP, and IP have done their work the data is sent to a networking device use to direct Internet traffic called a **router**. In home networks, routers are usually plugged into (or part of) a modem, this is the first router the newly made packets are sent. This personal router then sends the packets to the ISP's routers and from here they are send to many different routers along the "route" to the client. These packets are trying to find the fastest route possible, so if there is high traffic at one router, then it will take a different path. It is just like the roadways in the US, if there is a major accident or traffic jam, the cars (packets) will take a different road. The TCP/IP's job

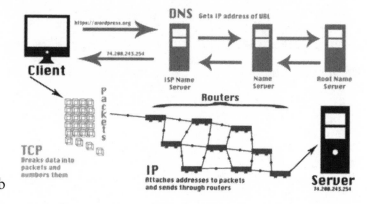

of numbering the packets and addressing is important in case some packets don't make the trip. This isn't uncommon, the client will just ask for the number packet it is missing instead of asking for the entire request. When the server gets these packets, it simply just does the same process in reverse.

First it collects the bits and turns them into packets, then IP arranges them into order and TCP turns the packets back into a message. The request is then processed and then sent back to the client the same way.

The Internet Infrastructure

The first step of the physical infrastructure of the Internet, as mentioned above, is the data getting sent to a router. These routers usually start with a local business or home router and then get sent to the ISP's router. For Internet provided over a cell signal (4G, LTE, etc.), the router is stored at the cell tower's location. Once it reaches the ISP's initial point of contact, it is then sent through several more routers that are connected to the previous router by one of three mediums: electricity, light, radio.

Electricity

One way to send these packets from one router to the next is by using copper wires. These copper wires send pulses the get converted in to 1's and 0's. Copper wire is found in most of the wires seen when connecting routers over a short distance and includes telephone wires (dial-up), DLS (another way to use telephone lines), and cable Internet (coaxial cables). While usually much faster than wireless, not nearly as fast as the speed of light.

Light

The fastest way to send these packets, especially long distances, is by using light in the form of fiber optic cables. Not only is using fiber optic cable faster, but it can also use a higher bandwidth and is not disturbed by electromagnetic interference. These fiber optic cables can consist of hundreds of individual fibers that can send light pulses that get converted back into 1's and 0's. In addition, different color lights at many different angles can be sent through the same fiber. While fiber optics is becoming more prevalent in large cities, it is most common in large underwater systems that connect continents. An interactive map of the cables resting at the bottom of oceans and where they connect to land can be seen on TeleGeography's Submarine Cable Map. Once the data reaches land, it travels from router to router until it arrives at the correct location. Since this data is traveling at the speed of light, it takes a fraction of a second to travel from Europe to the United States. Most of the girth of the cable is used to protect the hair-thin fibers that send the data thousands of miles in a split second.

Radio

The final way data is transferred is by radio waves. Radio waves are the part of the electromagnetic spectrum that range from 3 Hz to 3000 GHz. Some of these frequencies are used for things like AM radio, FM radio, television, satellite radio, microwaves, GPS, other forms of communication, and of course many Internet related transmissions. These frequencies are usually determined by a branch of the countries government, especially since some of the frequencies do not travel very far. Lower frequencies travel further since there is less electromagnetic interference and they can travel through objects better; but, with so many towers available nowadays, high frequencies are basically just as useful. All the U.S. frequency allocations are public and are provided by the U.S. Department of

Commerce. Most television, cell phone, GPS, Wi-Fi, Bluetooth, walkie-talkies, and cordless phones are found in the UHF (ultra-high frequency) range which spans 300 MHz to 3 GHz. The allocations are always changing with old technology becoming obsolete and new technology becoming more in-demand.

Speed

When sending digital data, everything is broken down to 1's and 0's or bits. The number of bits that can be processed per second is called the **bit rate**. The broader term **bandwidth** refers to the amount of recourses available to transmit the data and is usually measured in bit rate or frequency (higher frequency – lower frequency). **Latency** is sometimes defined as the amount of delay when sending digital data over the Internet, but is more commonly defined as the round-trip time information take to get from the client to the server and back. The latency is measured in milliseconds and can be found by pinging an IP address or URL, found in network preferences. Since this data is traveling at the speed of light, latency between North America and Europe is less than 50 milliseconds. In other words, fast.

Important Vocabulary

- **Network** – a group of computers that are connected so they can share resources using a data link
- **Internet** – a network of smaller networks connected using a specific set of rules that computers use to communicate with each other
- **IP** – Internet protocol, a unique address for every device connected to the Internet
- **IP Address** – a unique identifier for every device on the Internet
- **IPv4** – the version of IP that uses 32-bit addresses
- **IPv6** – the version of IP that uses 128-bit addresses
- **ISP** – Internet Service Provider
- **Protocol** – a specific set of rules
- **ARPANET** – the Advanced Research Projects Agency Network, first agency to use TCP/IP
- **Packets** – small chunks of data used in TCP/IP
- **Web** (World Wide Web) – the part of the Internet that uses HTTP and HTTPS
- **VoIP** – Voice over Internet Protocol, used for telephony
- **Server** – any computer that provides a service
- **Subdomain** – precedes the domain name, owned by the domain *https://subdomain.domain.com*

- **TCP** – Transmission Control Protocol, requests are broken down in to smaller, more manageable packets and numbered
- **UDP** – User Datagram Protocol, like TCP and usually used for streaming audio/video
- **URL** – Uniform Resource Locator, a specific file from a domain
- **Router** – a networking device that routes Internet traffic to the destination
- **Root Name Server** – one of 13 servers that contain every IP addresses and their matching domain names
- **POP** – Post Office Protocol, used for e-mail
- **Name Server** – a server that contains many IP addresses and their matching domain names
- **Latency** – the amount of delay when sending digital data over the Internet or the round-trip time information take to get from the client to the server and back
- **IMAP** – Internet Message Access Protocol, used for e-mail
- **HTTPS** – a secure version of HTTP that uses SSL/TLS
- **HTTP** – Hyper Text Transfer Protocol, used for websites
- **HTML** – Hyper Text Markup Language, the standard for creating web pages
- **FTP** – File Transfer Protocol, used for file transferring
- **Fault Tolerant** – a property of IP, if there is an error, it will still work properly

- **Domain Name** – a name given or linked to an IP address
- **DNS** – Domain Name System, one of the smaller networks that make up the Internet and contains many servers that act like phone books
- **Bandwidth** – the amount of recourses available to transmit the data
- **Client** – any computer that requests a service
- **Cloud Computing** – using a remote server to store files

Suggested Reading

- "You Can't Say That on the Internet." *Blown to Bits.* Chapter 7. Pages 229-257
- "Bits in the Air." *Blown to Bits.* Chapter 8. Pages 259-294
- "The Internet as System and Spirit." *Blown to Bits.* Appendix. Pages 301-316
- "Search Engine Indexing." *Nine Algorithms that Changed the Future.* Chapter 2. Pages 13-22
- "PageRank." *Nine Algorithms that Changed the Future.* Chapter 3. Pages 23-31

Unit 6 – HTML, CSS, and Adobe Dreamweaver

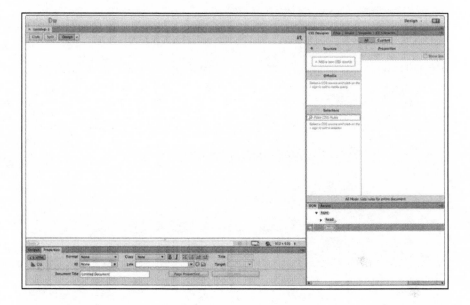

Intro to Adobe Dreamweaver

Adobe Dreamweaver (formerly Macromedia Dreamweaver) is a web development application originally created by Macromedia, and is now developed by Adobe Systems, which acquired Macromedia in 2005.

Dreamweaver is available for both Mac and Windows operating systems. Recent versions have incorporated support for web technologies such as CSS, JavaScript, and various server-side scripting languages and frameworks including ASP, ColdFusion, and PHP.

Creating a new website

Most every web page on the internet has more than one file contained in it; it might have multiple pages, pictures, style sheets, or other assets involved in it. When a website gets more complex, the number of files need to make it work also grow. To keep these files or assets organized, website will be folders on the computer with many subfolders containing many other files.

To create a new site, click *Site... New Site...* on the menu bar.

When the following window comes up, give the site a name next to '*Site Name:*', this is the name it will use inside of Dreamweaver and will not be seen anywhere on the actual website. Next, click the folder icon next to the text field labeled '*Local Site Folder:*'. This should be an empty folder created on your computer that can be created beforehand or when the folder icon is clicked.

Creating new pages

Once a site has been defined, a folder with all the files in the site will show up in the **Files** panel on the bottom right hand side of the screen. If this is a new site, then it will most likely be an empty folder. To add a new page to the site, right click on the folder and

select *New File*. If the new file is a web page, make sure the file extension is *.html*. New folders can also be created by right clicking. A new folder named *assets* should be created to four new folders: *images, css, fonts, js*. The will contain and

Local Files		Size	Type	Modified
▼ 📁 Site – About Me (Macint...			Folder	2/22/17 2:38 PM
▼ 📁 assets			Folder	1/18/17 10:44 AM
▼ 📁 css			Folder	1/18/17 10:44 AM
📄 syles.css		3KB	CSS File	2/7/17 10:35 AM
▶ 📁 images			Folder	1/18/17 11:07 AM
📄 index.html		4KB	HTML File	2/7/17 10:35 AM

CSS Designer | Files | Insert | Snippets | CC Libraries

About Me — Local view

images, style sheets, unique fonts, and JavaScript files respectively.

Views

At the top left of the file window, there are three buttons that let the user change the view of the website. These views are code, split, and design/live. Code shows the behind the scenes stuff, such as the html and css code and design/live shows what the page will look like in a web browser. Split lets both other views be open simultaneously. Sometimes it is easier to change content on a webpage in the design view, but the live view is helpful to get a better idea of how the site will respond in a webpage. Some CSS elements will not show up in the design view, nor will responsive webpages that change depending on the width of the page. Both design and live have their own advantages.

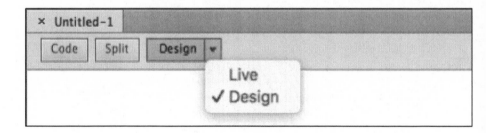

Properties Panel

The properties panel is located at the bottom of the screen and depending on what is selected on the page, different properties will be displayed. There are formatting options here for text, such as color and font. **Do not use these to change the look of text!** There will be many useful things that show up in the properties panel including links and page properties, but **not text formatting**, this will be done through CSS.

Adding Pictures and Links

To add a picture, simply save the image into the *images* folder and then drag the picture onto the page. The properties panel can be used to change the size, ID, source, class, alt tag, and more. There are also tool the modify this image, crop it, and even open it in Photoshop.

Links are also found on the properties panel. Simply copy and paste any URL into the text field labeled '*Link*'. If an existing webpage in the site is the desired link, the target symbol and be dragged to the HTML file or image in the '*Files*' tab or the folder icon can be clicked and the file can be selected that way. To have the link open in a new window or new tab, change the '*Target*' dropdown to the desired action.

Forms

The '*Form*' dropdown in the '*Insert*' tab is an easy way to access form elements, such as check boxes, text fields, radio buttons, checkboxes, buttons, and more all of which will be used in the JavaScript chapter of this book.

CSS

Cascading Style Sheets (CSS) is a style sheet language used to describe the presentation (that is, the look and formatting) of a document written in a markup language. The most common application is to style web pages written in HTML. CSS is designed primarily to enable the separation of document content (written in HTML or a similar markup language) from document presentation, including elements such as the colors, fonts, and layout. This separation can improve content accessibility, provide more flexibility and control in the specification of presentation characteristics, enable multiple pages to share formatting, and reduce complexity and repetition in the structural content (such as by allowing for table-less web design). CSS can also allow the same markup page to be presented in different styles for different rendering methods, such as on-screen, in print, specific devices, screen widths, screen resolution, and more. While the author of a document typically links that document to a CSS style sheet, readers can use a different style sheet, perhaps one on their own computer, to override the one the author has specified.

CSS specifies a priority scheme to determine which style rules apply if more than one rule matches against an element. In this so-called cascade, priorities or weights are calculated and assigned to rules, so that the results are predictable.

Rules
There are three general types of CSS rules: tag rules, class rules, and ID. While in the *'CSS Designer'* tab, click the plus sign next to the *'Selector'* section. This will automatically try and guess what is trying to be added by looking at what element is currently selected on the page. To change this, simply delete the text and write the desired rule.

The first type of rule is the **tag rule** which will redefine what an HTML tag looks like and include **body, h1, h2, h3, a, div, img,** and many more. The word tag here refers to the HTML tags in the document. There are over 90 known, but only a handful of tags that will be used often. The names of all the tag on an element can be seen at the bottom of the design view in the tag inspector bar (above the properties palette). The most common ones used are **body,** the heading tags (**h1-h6**), the anchor tag for links (**a**), **div** tags, the paragraph tag (**p**), and the image tag for pictures (**img**). These are just a few, when websites get more complex, more tags will be used. The **class rule** will be applied to any HTML tag that has that specific class on it and are always named **beginning with a period**. Once added to the CSS, these classes will show up in the '*Class*' dropdown found in the '*Properties*' panel. Class rules can be applied to any type and any number of HTML elements. They can even be added to small parts of elements like paragraphs or headings by automatically adding the <span> tags around the selection. Remember, the text formatting buttons should not be used, so class tags are the best way to bold, underline, or italicize things. Class tags can do countless things besides bold, underline, and italicize; such as put borders on tags, change font or background colors, align elements, add padding or margin, etc.

To add a rule to one specific element **ID rules** are used. Since ID's are unique names for elements, all ID's must be different. To add ID's to elements, find the *'ID'* text field in the *'Properties'* panel. To create the rule for the ID, name it **beginning with the pound/hash symbol (#)**. If the CSS rule for an ID is created without using that ID in the HTML, then that ID will show up in the dropdown section of the *'ID'* in the *"Properties"* panel.

There are also pseudo class selector rules, which include: link:, visited:, :hover, and :active. These are usually preceded by the *a* tag (i.e. - a: visited), but can be used on any tag (i.e. - h2: hover). These should be created in that order for links because of the cascading nature of CSS (the rules at the bottom of the list happen last). So, if hover was

All	Current

+ --- Properties

☐ Show Set

Layout

width	:	50 %
height	:	
min-width	:	
min-height	:	
max-width	:	
max-height	:	
display	:	
box-sizing	:	

margin : Set Shorthand

0 px

auto   auto

0 px

padding : Set Shorthand

40 px

40 px   40 px

40 px

position :

top: auto

left: auto   right: auto

bottom: auto

above visited in the CSS, then hover would only work if the link had not been visited yet because visited happens after hover.

Rules inside of rules can also be used in the advanced rule such as **div #container h1**. This would only be applied to an h1 tag inside of a div tag with the ID container. If the same property needs to be added to multiple elements, they can be named and separated by common: **#container, h1, h2, .highlight.**

Defining CSS Rules

Now that the different kinds of CSS rules have been stated, what kinds of things can they do?

There are five sections on the right-hand 'CSS Designer' Property panel that will jump down to the corresponding section of the menu: Layout, Text, Border, Background,

More. Many of the menus are self-explanatory: type is the font for the specific rule, background is the background, and border is the border around the rule. There is also a *'Show Set'* checkbox in the top right corner of this panel; if his is checked, then only the styles being used will been seen. To see all styles, make sure this box is unchecked.

A commonly used property in are margin and padding. These modify the box, which is an invisible box around all tags and is very useful when sizing and laying out the webpage. The box can easily be seen if a border or background is added to the rule.

By default, the tags width is 100% of the page and its height is only as tall as needed to fit the material. These can be change using width and height under the box menu. Float is what side of the page the tag is aligned to (left by default). Padding refers to the inside of the box and how close things are to the inside edge (think of a padded cell, keep the person inside away from the hard wall). Margin is the outside edge of the box and set how close other tags can come to it.

@Media Queries

In addition to using CSS to change the look of the page, it can also be used to change the look of many other media queries. These

include conditions that will check to see if the user is looking at a print preview, if they are in landscape or portrait mode on a tablet or cell phone, what their screen resolution is, and many more including the most import one, max-width. Max-width will check to see how wide their screen is and use the defined styles for that width. This is very important in designing responsive website that respond to the device that is being used. A large desktop display and a mobile phone should not look the same. For example, there will be little or no padding on cell phones since real estate is scarce on such a small screen. Also, images might be different sizes on cell phones or maybe taken out altogether.

To add these media queries, simply click the plus sign next to '@Media' in the 'CSS Designer' panel. In this pop-up box, there will be at least one drop-down menu for any given condition. Multiple conditions can be added by clicking the plus sign that will show up when the current condition is hovered over. This is useful for something like defining what a website look like that is both in landscape mod AND aspect-ratio is specific size. Once the media query is added, just add styles while clicked on the new media query. The cascading property of CSS will make sure the new styles take effect since they are below the others in the style sheet.

A common set of break points are devices larger than 1200 pixels (large desktops), between 992 pixels and 1199 pixels (regular desktops and tablets in landscape mode), between 768 pixels and 991 pixels (most tablets in portrait mode), and smaller than 767 pixels (most smart phones). When these are added to the media query, they can visually be seen in the live view (see above image) at the top of the page.

When viewing a website on a desktop, the content should move all over the place when the size of the window is changed. To avoid this, a container div tag (simply a div tag surrounding everything in the site with the ID: container) with a set width is use on the largest two screen sizes (i.e. – width: 950px). Since the screen sizes of tablet and smartphones cannot be changed, it is appropriate to use the percent of the screen when setting the width of a container div tag (i.e. – width: 90%). It is also important to note that margins and padding will affect the percentage of a tag. This means that is a div tag is set to 100% and other elements around it have padding or margin, the width might be more than 100% of the page. Make sure the page cannot scroll to the left or right to make sure more than 100% is not being used.

Bootstrap

Bootstrap is the most popular HTML, CSS, and JS framework for developing responsive, mobile first projects on the web and was originally created by a designer and a

developer at Twitter, Bootstrap has become one of the most popular front-end frameworks and open source projects in the world. Bootstrap was originally released in August of 2011 and since has had over twenty releases. Version 3 rewrote the library to make it responsive by default with a mobile first approach.

The entire framework (as well as all the documentation) can be found and downloaded at *getbootstrap.com*. The download contains everything needed to start a site, including CSS files, JavaScript files, and fonts (including glyphicons). Luckily, Dreamweaver already has all this information stored, so by choosing the **Bootstrap** tab under *'New Document'* → *'HTML'*. It is important to have already set-up the website (site... new site from earlier in this chapter), otherwise all the assets will be save in whatever the most recent file's folder is. Uncheck the *'Include a pre-built layout'* checkbox to start fresh.

All the Bootstrap files and folders should now be seen in the *'File'* tab. This includes a css folder with a read only bootstrap.css file, a fonts folder with various files, and a js folder with a couple JavaScript files. To get the index.html page in the root folder, simply click file save and rename the blank html page as index.html, it should already be in the correct folder.

Since the CSS file is read only, it cannot be modified, this is intentional. Since style sheets cascade, a new style sheet can be created below the read only one. To do this click the plus sign next to *'Sources'* in the *'CSS Designer'* tab and select *'Create A New CSS*

File', save this into the folder appropriately named css. This is where styles can be created or overwritten, an appropriate name for this file could be custom.css.

Once all Bootstrap files are set-up, Bootstrap Components can be added to the blank HTML page (remember to work in the 'live' view to best see these components). A list of the components can be found on the *'Inset'* tab's drop-down menu under *'Bootstrap Components'*.

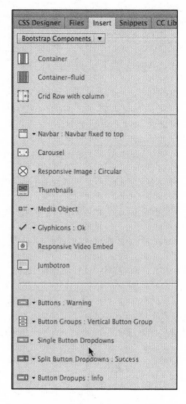

These components can be added by dragging them in to the body in the live view, but may not respond the desired way. Do drag a component into another component or tag (div, p, h1, etc.), drag and hover over the element until the inside edges glow blue. To put the component before or after the element, look for a green bar while hovering. Again, these might not act the desired way or be placed in the desired position.

To better place components, select the element above or below where it should go and click (not drag) the component. A pop-up will show up giving options to place the new component before, after, nested, and sometimes wrapped around the selected element. Likewise, it may be easier to place components in the correct place by dragging over the </> symbol and using the DOM representation of the page.

Unit 7 – Big Data and Security

Big Data

Data is everywhere and has been collected for multiple purposes since the beginning of time. This data started out to be simple, like when and where cavemen could find food to tribes tracking weather patterns. With advancing technologies, data has become easier to collect and used for many more reasons. In the last 50 years, tracking what television programs people watched have led to the current state of TV and targeted advertising. With this data, companies and advertising agencies can better target consumers that are interested in their products. This saves these companies millions of dollars by not wasting money on consumers who, most likely, will not buy their product and increasing sales by targeting the 'more likely to buy' consumers.

Big data often refers to sets of data that are larger than a consumer software application can handle. This could be data collected from hundreds of sources, but with today's technology includes mobile phones, software, web browser logs, cameras, and wireless networks. A few key features about big data are the volume of the data, the rate at which it is collected, the variety of types, and the fact computers can 'learn' from it. The volume is important since it is not a sample of data from different groups of people, it is all the data from all the people so there is less room for error. The rate at which data is collected is also important since, with the speed of processors and fiber optics, the data is in real-time. The variety of big data allows text, audio, video, and more to all be collected simultaneously and analyzed. This allows the data to be seen from different angles, making the results even more accurate. Finally, computers can see trends and patterns from this data that would take humans a life time to sift through even a small percent of it. Not only can computers see the trends, but they can also learn from it and use it when seeing similar data in the future. Big data is very powerful and companies pay top dollar to obtain it.

In 2012 Facebook bought Instagram for $1 Billion. That is a billion, with a 'B'. Any programmer at Facebook could easily have designed an app that did the exact same thing as Instagram and probably improved it. So why pay one-thousand million dollars for an app? At the time, Instagram had 30 million users and it also had a lot of data about those 30 million users. Data that included how often they were on the app, how long they used the app per session, what profiles they looked at, what pictures they liked, all there search results, and more. The app itself was not worth $1 Billion, but the large set of data Instagram collected and their daily active users were worth that much to Facebook.

Big data is seen in many other industries including government, education, media, healthcare, banking, real estate, banking, retail, and more. The app Waze uses every user's data, even when the app is not open. When installed, the user gives permission to always use their location. If the user's geolocation in on a road, then the app can record their speed. This can predict traffic and help re-route other users in real-time.

Security

With all this sensitive and valuable data being transferred every second, it is important to keep it secure. You probably would not yell your social security number or credit card number across a crowded room. In the same way, you should not send this data through unsecure methods. There are several ways that security **hackers**, someone who exploits weaknesses on a computer or network, can steal or disrupt data. Some of these hackers just want to harm or break a network and others want to gather this data for other purposes, like identity theft or obtaining credit card numbers.

One way hackers can perform these malicious tasks is by installing a **virus** on a computer or server. A virus is a program that infects other programs and usually spreads to other programs or computers by copying itself repeatedly. Most virus are a result of the user. This could happen by opening an email attachment from an unknown source or even just plugging in a USB drive to the computer. Once the virus is installed, it is hard to remove since it masks itself as other programs. Luckily, today's anti-virus software can catch most of these threats.

Another was hackers try and obtain this data is by **phishing** or using "bait" to trick the user into entering sensitive information like user names, passwords, or credit card numbers. Hackers create a fake site or email that looks identical to a trustworthy website and try to get the user to log-in or update info. Instead of logging-in to the real site, the info is sent directly to the hackers who can easily test your user name and password combination into hundreds of other sites in a matter of seconds. Two ways the user can protect themselves are by always making sure the URL is the correct URL for the real site. Any site can add a subdomain to the beginning of their URL, so https://amazon.com and http://amazon.ft543ffj.com (the actual site is ft543ffj.com) are completely different domains. The second way users can protect themselves is by making sure they never use the same password for more than one website.

Password strength is equally as important. Many users think if they use a number and a symbol in their password, then it is hard to crack. This is not the case, the main way to increase the strength of the password is by making it longer. Hackers compile a list of passwords they find every time there is data stolen. If any password is on that list, it would take no time at all to break into user accounts. The hackers can even test all these passwords to see if there is an at sign (@) in place of an A or a dollar sign ($) in place of an S, these do not help password strength. Since length is the main indicator of a strong password, something like *"Bhdiu3fbEieef$nei3rf"* would be great, but it is doubtful anyone would memorize a password like that for every site they visit. Password management sites, like 1Password.com, can be used to generate these random passwords and store them. Another technique is to combine four words into one long word and making one of the words obscure is even better. So, a great password that is easier to remember than random characters could be *"paperelephantchartreusecoconut"*. This is even longer than the previous example and much easier to remember. By making this the password for a password management site and having that site store different, long, and random sets of characters for all other site is a good practice and only one password needs to be memorized.

Another method hackers use to cause havoc to a website is by using a **distributed denial-of-service attack (DDoS)**. In this method, hackers flood a site with fake request making all the site's recourses unavailable for legitimate users. This method does not steal any information or try to install any viruses, it simple hurts the site's business. There are many possible motives for a DDoS attack including spite, revenge, blackmail, and others. There are many defenses to a DDoS attack, like blocking certain IP address and firewalls.

Cryptography

Cryptography is often referred to as **encryption**, which is simply taking text and converting it so it is illegible. The reverse process, or converting the illegible text back into legible text, is known as **decryption**. To be able to encrypt and decrypt data, a list of instructions is needed. A **cipher** is a pair of **algorithms** (the list of instructions) that give details on how to encrypt and decrypt the data. There is also a shared secret, or **key**, that is needed to make the difficulty of the encryption harder to crack. This key is usually a string of characters and can be known publicly to the users or it can be private (which allows it to be sent over unsecure methods).

Types of Ciphers

One famous cipher is the **Caesar Cipher** or Caesar shift where each letter is shifted the same amount. So, if the shift (or key) was set to 1, then 'A' would become 'B', 'R' would become 'S', 'X' would become 'Y', and 'Z' would loop around to the beginning of the alphabet and become 'A'. If the shift was 10, it would move each letter 10 places ahead and 'A' would become 'K'. To decrypt the message, simply shift the key backwards.

Example:

>**Key:** 14
>
>**Plain text:** Computer Science is fun
>
>**Encrypted text:** Qcadihsf Gqwsbqs wg tib

This is a very simple cipher to use, but because of the patterns of letters, makes it simple to crack or decipher. With computers, it would be solved in a split second.

Another simple encryption example is the **random substitution cipher.** In this cipher, a letter is mapped or swapped with another letter in the alphabet. So, 'A' could be mapped to 'F', 'B' could be mapped to 'Z', 'C' could be mapped to 'A', and so on until all 26 letters were mapped to another letter.

Example:

ABCDEFGHIJKLMNOPQRSTUVWXYZ

Key: SGPFNEYQUJKRCDVMIZAXHWOLBT

Plain text: Computer Science is fun

Encrypted text: Pvcmhxnz ua ehd

This seem much harder to crack than the Caesar cipher, but it also has patterns, which makes it easy to break. This can be done quickly by a computer, but can also be done by hand by looking at reoccurring sets of letters and frequency of letters. The letter 'E' is the most common letter in the English language, so whatever letter shows up most in the encrypted text is probably mapped to 'E'. If the same three letter appear multiple times, this could be the word "the", solving three letters at once.

A more difficult cipher to crack is the **Vigenère cipher**, which has similarities to the Caesar cipher and dates to the 1460's. Like in the Caesar cipher, the Vigenère cipher uses a key to set the amount of letters the message will shift, but in the Vigenère cipher, the key is much longer and not the same for every letter. If the key was a phrase like "applesaretasty", then the first 14 characters would shift according to what letter was in the key at that place. The first letter would shift by 'A' or 1, the second and third by 'P' or 16 and so on. The fifteenth letter would just start back at the beginning of the key and repeat itself until the whole text was encrypted.

Even though this is difficult to crack, it still can rely on patterns and letter frequencies to find the key. The only way to make this unbreakable would be to have a key that was longer than the text itself, removing any patterns that arise.

Example (assuming '_' is the 27th letter):

Key: APPLESARETASTY

Plain text: COMPUTER_SCIENCE_IS_FUN

Encrypted text:

CCA_YKEHDKC_XKCTOTWRFKR

A famous example of breaking ciphers and decrypting message can be seen in the film *The Imitation Game*. This is the true story about Alan Turing, an English mathematician (would be called a Computer Scientist today) who helped crack the German **Enigma machine** during World War II and shortened the war by several years by being able to read the encrypted German messages. A YouTube search will show exactly how the machine worked and how it was eventually cracked.

Public Key Encryption

When talking about encryption, it is common to use two people communicating with one person (or an eavesdropper) listening in. These two people are usually named **Alice** and **Bob** with the "spy" named **Eve**. To use any of the previous cipher examples a shared key is needed that no one else know, hence the name **private key**. If Alice and Bob both know the private key and Eve does not, then encryption and decryption are simple. Eve will not be able to read the message between Alice and Bob, even if she intercepts it. Without the private key, the message just looks like jumbled characters. Since Alice and Bob both use the sane key to encrypt and decrypt the message, it is known **as symmetric key encryption**. This is a great way to send secret messages, but the problem is obtaining the private key. What if Alice is in New York and Bob is in Tokyo? If they try and send the key to each other, then Eve can intercept it and decrypt any messages sent in the future.

Public key encryption is a system that allows Alice and Bob to publicly publish a key that everyone, including Eve, can see. The best way to think about public key is by using padlocks. Adding Bob's public key encryption to a message is like putting a padlock on the message that only Bob has the key to. So, if Alice want to send an encrypted message to Bob, she encrypts it with Bob's public key. Only Bob has the information needed to unlock the "padlock" and read the message. Since the encryption key is different than the decryption key, public key encryption is also known as **asymmetric key encryption**.

How Public Key Works

Public key encryption creates a problem that is computationally hard, like in the Travelling Salesman dilemma in Unit 4. A computer could crack the cipher, but it would take several super computers hundreds or even thousands of years. Even though public key is tough to break, it is very simple to use. A problem that is easy in one

direction and difficult in the other is known as a **one-way function.**
Another one-way function, that is used in public key as well, is clock
or **modular arithmetic.** Imagine an analog clock was set to 12 noon
and then someone moved the hour hand ahead to 3 o'clock. This
might appear that the hour hand was only moved ahead 3 hours, but
it could have been moved ahead a full rotation plus 3 hours which is
15 hour or 2 full rotations plus 3 hours which is 27 hours. It could
have been moved ahead an infinite number of rotation plus 3 hours,
it is impossible to know. The only person who has this information
is the person that moved the clock ahead. This is easy for the person
moving the clock, but impossible for anyone who does not know
how many rotations were made. In a very broad way, this is how
public key encryption works

Types of Public Key Encryption
Two of the most commonly used public key encryption algorithms
are **Diffie-Hellman** (named after Whitefield Diffie and Martin
Hellman) and **RSA** (named after Ron Rivest, Adi Shamir, Leonard
Adleman). Diffie-Hellman was one of the first public key encryption
protocols and dates to the mid-1970s. Diffie-Hellman is considered a
key exchange algorithm, a way to swap the private key needed for
other encryption algorithms.

RSA followed Diffie-Hellman and in addition to asymmetric
encryption, it also allows for **digital signature.** The digital signature

is an electronic signature that, by using public key, can be verified authentic. Both these algorithms are integral in security today.

Public Key Security Certificates

Another application of public key encryption is seen when browsing the web. It is important to trust the website being vested and to also have a secure connection so Eve cannot see what is being communicated between the user and the site. This is happening every time **https://** is used. The 's' stands for secure and is using the Diffie-Hellman key exchange, RSA, or others to secure the connection through a **digital handshake**. This process is referred to as **Transport Layer Security (TLS)** and its predecessor was **Secure Sockets Layer (SSL)**. Even though TLS is the newer protocol, it is still referred to as simply SSL, but TLS is being used. Public key is used in SSL by authenticating a **Digital Certificate**, a trusted third-party file that shows the site is verified and legit. When possible, always use SSL (https) when visiting websites. There are plug-ins available in some web browsers that always force https over http.

Important Vocabulary
- **Big Data** – sets of data that are larger than a consumer software application can handle
- **Hacker** – someone who exploits weaknesses on a computer or network and can steal or disrupt data

- **Virus** – a program that infects other programs and usually spreads to other programs or computers by copying itself repeatedly

- **Phishing** – using "bait" to trick the user into entering sensitive information like user names, passwords, or credit card numbers

- **DDoS** – distributed denial-of-service attack, hackers flood a site with fake request making all the site's recourses unavailable for legitimate users

- **Encryption** – taking text and converting it so it is illegible

- **Decryption** – the reverse process of encryption

- **Cipher** – is a pair of algorithms that give details on how to encrypt and decrypt the data

- **Caesar Cipher** – a shift cipher where each letter is shifted the same amount

- **Digital signature** – an electronic signature that, by using public key, can be verified authentic

- **Digital Certificate** – a trusted third-party file that shows the site is verified and legit

- **Asymmetric key encryption** – a different key is used to encrypt and decrypt a message

- **Key** – in cryptography, a shared secret to make the difficulty of the encryption harder to crack

- **Modular arithmetic** – using the remainder when dividing, also known as clock arithmetic
- **One-way Function** - a problem that is easy in one direction and difficult in the other
- **Private Key** – a shared secret to help decrypt a message
- **Public Key** – a system that allows a key to be publicly published
- **SSL** – Secure Sockets Layer, issues digital certificates for websites
- **Substitution cipher** – a cipher where a letter is mapped or swapped with another letter in the alphabet
- **Symmetric key encryption** – the same key is used to encrypt and decrypt a message
- **TLS** – Transport Layer Security, issues digital certificates for websites

Suggested Reading
- "Secret Bits." *Blown to Bits.* Chapter 5. Pages 161-193
- "Public Key Cryptography." *Nine Algorithms that Changed the Future.* Chapter 4. Pages 32-46
- "Digital Signatures." *Nine Algorithms that Changed the Future.* Chapter 9. Pages 109-125

Unit 8 – Programming: Java

History and Usage

JavaScript was originally developed by Brendan Eich of Netscape Communications Corporation and was first introduced in December of 1995. JavaScript is a scripting language with a syntax loosely based on C and like C, it has reserved keywords. Also like C, the language has no input or output constructs of its own. Where C relies on standard I/O libraries, a JavaScript engine relies on a host environment into which it is embedded, in our case a web browser.

Since JavaScript cannot stand alone (it needs a web browser to run), many consider it a scripting language and not a programming language, but JavaScript should still be considered a **high-level language**. High level languages (C, Java, Python, etc.) differ from low-level languages (binary, assembly, machine language, etc.) in that they are easy to read by humans, which make them easier to debug. High-level languages also rely on abstraction and other libraries that already exist. These high-level languages get turned into low-level languages before the get to the hardware using a compiler or interpreter.

ebugging

Depending on the development environment, debugging could prove to be quite difficult. Since errors in JavaScript only appear in run-time (i.e., there is no way to check for errors without executing the code) and since JavaScript is interpreted by the web browser as the page is viewed, it may be difficult to track the cause for errors. Today, however, web browsers come with reasonably good debuggers. Since the arrival of integrated toolbars and plug-ins, an increasing amount of support for JavaScript debugging is becoming readily available.

Scripting languages are especially susceptible to bugs for the inexperienced programmer. Because JavaScript is interpreted, loosely-typed, and has varying environments (host applications), implementations, and versions, the programmer should take exceptional care to make sure the code executes as expected.

Development Process

In computer programming, the process of creating and developing software should take be both iterative and incremental. It should be **incremental** in that it is done in small chunks and **iterative** in that it continuously repeats these steps. The main steps in this process are **Design – Implement – Test**. The **design phase** consists of brainstorming and prototyping and is the most creative step of the process. The **implement phase** is putting the design into code and since the design is already set, it should be the least creative phase. The **test phase** is checking to see if the code runs properly and finding errors or debugging the program. Since this process is iterative, the design phase comes after the test phase and the program is constantly updated and improved. This process is seen every time a new version of software is released.

JavaScript

To insert JavaScript into HTML, you must use the <SCRIPT> tag. To close this tag when the JavaScript is complete, you need to use the </SCRIPT> tag. JavaScript should be placed somewhere within the body of the HTML code, depending upon when the programmer wants to display their JavaScript program.

Like HTML, the computer does not read white space in JavaScript; most commands in JavaScript, therefore, need to end in a semicolon to tell the computer when one command ends and another begins. JavaScript also used the three basic logic structures in programming: sequence, selection, iteration. **Sequence** is the structure that runs one line after another, without skipping or repeating code. So, after line 1 comes line 2 and after line 1001 comes line 1002.

Comments can be used to let the programmer, and anyone who looks at their code, know what exactly is going on. The programmer can more clearly define variables and what they are trying to accomplish in certain areas of the program. These are especially helpful when going back to older projects after not looking at them for an extended period.

Using Variables

Variables are a way to store information to the computer. Variables can store many kinds of data, such as text and numbers. Before variables can be used, they must first be defined. The keyword *var* is used in JavaScript to setup a new variable. The word following *var* is going to be the name of the new variable. The programmer may name this variable anything they would like. The name they choose should be relevant to what it is storing. For example: if the programmer is storing a string of text that says "Hello, how are you doing today?", then the variable might be called *greeting*, if it is storing someone's last name it might be called *lastName*. Notice that *lastName* is one word, no variables can have spaces nor can they start with anything but a letter. Also, the letter l in *lastName* is lower case, and the N is upper case. This is called camel casing because the first letter is lower case and every new word is upper case. This is one way to avoid spaces; the underscore is another way: *last_name*. We will practice camel casing at various points in class.

var greeting;

This line of code creates a variable name greeting that has nothing stored to it yet.

Strings

One thing a variable can store is a string, which is another way of saying text. A string may contain any character on the keyboard (even the space bar counts as a character). A string can be identified because it is surrounded by quotation marks. "Hello, how are you?" is an example of such a string. To create a string, the programmer must use quotation marks. Also, any input that is received from a prompt is in string form, even numbers.

greeting = "Hello, how are you?";

This line of code assigns the string "Hello, how are you?" to the variable greeting.

Both creating the variable and assigning the variable can be combined into one step:

var greeting = "Hello, how are you?";

Numbers

A number differs from a string in that a string cannot be multiplied, rounded, or have any other mathematical operation applied to them. Another important difference is that unlike strings, numbers do not have quotes around them.

var myAge = 17;

This creates a variable named *myAge* and assigns the value 17 to it.

Alerts

The programmer can send a message to the user before they can access the webpage. In JavaScript, this is called an alert; it pops up in a dialog box on the webpage. To do this, use the alert command:

alert("This is an alert!");

Notice the parentheses contain a string; they could also contain a number or a variable. Whatever is written in the parentheses will be

This page says:

This is an alert!

OK

displayed in the alert. Also, the command must end in a semicolon to let the program know it is finished.

A variable can also be placed inside the parentheses. Remember there are no quotes around a variable!

alert(greeting);

Prompts

Prompts are like alerts in that they pop up with a dialog box. The difference with prompts is that they are going to ask the user for input. Since there is input coming into the program, it should be stored somewhere.

This page says:

Enter your input

☐ Prevent this page from creating additional dialogs.

type here

Cancel   OK

Recall that variables are used to store items and that all inputs are stored as strings. The *prompt("Enter input: ", "Default Text");* is going to return whatever the user enters into the prompt. To store the input, therefore, let's assign a variable to this prompt:

var userInput = prompt("Enter your input", "type here");

Concatenation

To combine two stings together, concatenation must be used. Concatenation is the combination of two strings. To concatenate two strings in JavaScript, the "+" sign must be used. This can be used as many times as needed in the program:

alert("Hello " + username + "how are you?");

Converting String into Numbers

Remember that any input to the program is stored as a string. When a user inputs something into a prompt, it is stored as a string. This is a problem if a number is entered into the prompt. For example, if 17 is entered into the prompt, it will be stored as "17", a string. Math cannot be applied to a string; it must be converted into a number. The command to do this is *parseInt( );* and *parseFloat( );* for integers and floating point (decimals) respectively. Again, this returns a number, so it must be stored somewhere. The programmer probably does not need to keep the string "17" stored, so whatever variable it was stored as can be saved over:

var userAge = prompt("What is your age?", "Enter age here");
userAge = parseInt(userAge);

The string that is to be converted into a number is inside the parentheses. The *userAge* on the left side of the second line is the new number, and the one in the parentheses is a string.

Basic Math Operations

Now that there are numbers stored, mathematics can be applied to them. First, set up a new variable to store the solution and then assign the math to that variable. Addition (+), subtraction (-), multiplication (*), and division (/) can all be used here.

    var dogAge = userAge * 7;

This creates a new variable called *dogAge* and sets it to the user's age multiplied by 7.

Selection

Sometimes it is not necessary to run all the script on the webpage. There might be times when there are certain conditions that need to be met to run a block of code. For example, if the user inputs their age, there could be a different alert for kids, teenagers, and adults. If the user inputs an age below 13, he or she gets one message, between 14 and 17 gets another message, and everyone 18 and older gets another. This allows the computer to decide between multiple cases, called **selection** in computer programming. Selection, along with sequence and iteration are the three logic structures in programming.

If Statements

The way to give separate selections depending on the user's age can be accomplished by using **if statements**. An **if** statement begins with the word "if" (notice the lower case i) and the condition that needs to be met follows inside the parentheses. Conditions use the following symbols:

<	Less than
>	Greater than
<=	Less than or equal to
>=	Greater than or equal to
==	Equal to
!=	Not equal to

After the parenthesis is closed around the conditional statement, braces { } are opened. **Notice: There is no semi-colon after the parenthesis is closed!** Anything that comes between these braces is what will be executed if the conditional statement is true. If the conditional statement is not true, the code in the braces will be ignored.

A snippet of the code for the age program might look something like this:

```
if ( age <= 12 )
{
        alert("Enjoy your youth while it lasts!");
}
```

Else if statements

If another **if** statement is used (usually conditions with the same variable), an **else if** can be used—this will connect the statements together. If the first **if** statement is true, then the **else if** statement will be ignored. The order of the statements matter, therefore. These statements are exactly like **if** statements, except for the word else before them.

This example might follow the snippet from above:

```
else if ( age <= 17 )
{
        alert("Not too long before you can vote!");
}
```

Since the **if** statement above covers the ages 12 and below, this statement will only cover the ages from 13 to 17. Why you ask?

Well, if the age is 12 or below, the first **if** statement will be true, and it will never get to the **else if** statement. There can be unlimited **else if** statements in the code.

Else statements

The else statement can be used for any condition that is not met using the **if** or **else if** statements. The **else** statement is a little different than the others because it does not need a conditional statement. This is because it will only happen if the other statements are not true. In the age example, the **else** statement could look like this:

else

{

   alert("You are so old now!");

}

There can only be one **else** statement connected to each **if** statement, but the **else** statement is not necessary, nor is the **else if**.

Notice: There cannot be else if or else statements without an if statement!

Switch Statements

The switch statement is like the **if** statement with the major difference being that the switch statement will run a segment of code for different cases. For example, the user might be asked to pick a number from a menu, the switch statement lets the programmer run different code depending on the user's input. This could be done with **if** statements, but it is much simpler with the switch.

The switch starts with the command:

> *switch*(someVariable*)*
>
> *{*

Notice: The block is opened with the open brace {   (not a parenthesis)

The *someVariable* is usually the variable that the user inputs. This variable can be anything from a single letter or number to a word or phrase. After the opening brace, the variable is compared and the appropriate code is run. In the switch, each option the programmer puts to be tested is called a *case.* To set up a case, simply write *case* followed by the desired input. If this desired input is a word or letter, then it must be in quotation marks (unless you are using an existing variable); numbers do not have to have such marks. A colon follows this to tell the computer that the code to run is beginning. There can be as much or as little code as needed. To tell the computer the code is ending, the line *break;* is used. Without *break;*, the computer will not know the next case is beginning. Here are a few examples:

Example 1:

```
case 1:
        alert("You have picked choice number 1!");
        alert("You can have as much code as needed
here...");
        break;
```

Example 2:

```
case "yes":
        alert("You enter yes.");
        //all the code needed
        //even more code if necessary
break;
}       //when all cases are complete, make sure to close the
        //switch statement with a close brace
```

If there is something that the programmer wants to happen if none of the cases are met, then the *default* case should be used. Instead of the word *case* followed by a case, simply write the word *default* followed by a semicolon. Remember JavaScript is case sensitive.

```
default:
        alert("None of the cases were met!");
```

Notice that the default case is not followed by the line *break*. Since this case must be the last one, it does not need to tell the computer a new case is about to begin.

Iteration

Iteration means to repeat a process and in programming this is accomplished by using loops. A **loop** is a block of code that the programmer wants to run more than once. The number of times this loop is run could be different in every situation. The loop might need to be run an exact number of times (ex: ten, one hundred, etc.), or the loop might need to be run until a certain condition is met, like until a counter reaches a number or until the user picks the correct answer to a question. Two kinds of loops are *for* loops and *while* loops.

For Loops

for loops are the loops that are used to run a loop an exact number of times. *For* loops have three parts: the user must first initialize a counter variable, he or she must set a condition for the loop to keep executing, and he or she must set in what increment the counter changes. The first part initializes a counter and the most common name for this variable is *i*. The next part is a condition that tells the loop how long to run—this would include the variable that was just initialized. It might look like this: $i < 10$. This means if *i* is less than ten, the loop will continue to execute. The final part of this loop is the increment—this loop tells how much to increase or decrease the counter variable. If the programmer wants to increase the loop by 5 every time it executes, then he or she would type: $i = i + 5$;. To decrease by 20 every time, the programmer would use: $i = i - 20$; and so on. Since increasing and decreasing the counter by 1 is so common, there is a short hand way to write it: $i++$ and $i--$. These three steps are contained in one set of parentheses, and each of the steps is separated by semicolons. The block of code that is to be run in every loop is contained in braces. Together these parts look like this:

```
for( var i = 1; i < 10; i++ )
{
        Code to be run over and over goes here...
}
```

While Loops

A *while* loop is kind of like a simpler *for* loop. *While* loops only have one part to them: the condition. This means that the programmer must set up a variable and make sure the condition is eventually met. An example of a *while* loop is asking the user for a password. While the user guesses the incorrect password, the loop continues to run, not letting user continue with the rest of the code.

```
var myPassword = "12345";
var userGuess = " ";
while( userGuess != myPassword)
{
        userGuess = prompt("Enter the password");
}
```

This code sets up two variables, one for the actual password and one for the user's guess. Notice the user's guess is just setup as an empty string; the user has not guessed anything yet. Next, the while loop has a condition that says if the user's guess and the password are not equal, the loops continue. Inside the loop is simply a prompt that asks the user to enter a password.

Getting Stuck in Loops

The most common error with loops is using a condition that is always true. One case of this is if the programmer sets up a *for* loop that starts at 1, whose condition is $i < 10$, and decrements i by one every time. If i loses one every time, then the condition of $i < 10$ is **always** going to be true and therefore the loop will never end. If the computer gets stuck in a loop two things might happen: 1.) there might be an alert that never goes away causing the user to exit the program, 2.) the computer tries repeatedly to carry out something that will never happen and tells the user the program is not responding. Make sure the loops are not endless before executing the program.

Multiple Conditions

Inside things with conditions, like if statements and loops, the programmer might want to have a case where more than one condition needs to be met or at least one condition of many is met. Here the **&& (AND)** and **|| (OR)** symbols can be used. The **&** symbol is found above (hold down the shift key) the 7 key and the | symbol is found above the \ key (which is found between the backspace and enter keys). If there is a situation where a variable called age need to be between 18 and 25 the code might look like this:

if (age >= 18 && age <= 25)

If the situation called for the age to be either younger than 18 or 55 or older this code would be used:

if (age < 18 || age >= 55)

As many of these connectors can be used in a single conditional statement, like the following code:

while (age == 18 && weight < 400 && height > 42 &&
hair == "blonde" && eyes == "blue")

Objects and Methods

JavaScript is an object-based programming language, which means that certain items in the language are stored as objects and each of these objects has specific characteristics. Five important objects used in JavaScript are the **Math** object, the **document** object, the **string** object, the **Date** object, and the **array** object. Each of these objects "has" two features: *properties* and *methods.*

There are two different kinds of objects, objects that need to be set up by creating a new variable and those that can be used by simply saying the name of the object. The *new* keyword is used to create a new object to store in a variable, the *new* keyword needs to be used in the **date** and **array** objects; these will be discussed later in detail. The **string** object needs to be saved as a variable too, but the *new* keyword is not necessary. The **Math** and the **document** objects are both the type of objects where no variable needs to be set up, simply say Math or document when using these objects. Notice that **Math** is capitalized and **document** is all lowercase, JavaScript is CASE SENSITIVE.

Properties hold information about the object. In the **string** *and* the **array** object, one property is *length*, which holds the length of the string or array. In the **Math** object *PI* is a property that holds the value of Π (approx. 3.14). In the **document** object, some properties are *bgColor, fgColor,* and *title.* The **document** object talks about the actual webpage, so *bgColor* holds the background color, *fgColor* holds the foreground color, and the *title* is the title of the page. There are many others that can be found using a simple web search.

Methods are something the object can do. In the Math object, there are many methods, such as *sin, cos, tan, round, random, abs,* and *floor.* These methods *do* something to a number. They don't just hold information like properties do. In the string object, there are the methods *toUpperCase* and *toLowerCase.* These take a string and *do* something to them; they either make them into all upper or lower case letters. In the document object, there are the *open, write,* and *close* methods. Here the *open* method *does* something by opening the HTML file so that the file can be written to using the *write* method. After the programmer is done writing to the HTML document, it needs to be closed using the *close* method. In the date object the important methods are *getDay, getDate, getMonth, getHours,* *getMinutes,* and *getSeconds.* These methods retrieve information as a number about the specified part of the date. The finally object, the array object, has many methods as well. Some of the common array methods include *join, sort, concat,* and *reverse.* These methods will be addressed deeper into this chapter.

String Methods

Just like numbers, strings may be manipulated in JavaScript. One common way to manipulate a string is to change it to all upper-case letters. To do this, we must call a method. Methods will be discussed in more detail later. To use this method, there must first be a string variable, which is just a variable with a string stored in it. *stringVar* will be the variable in this example. The period (.) is the way to call, or carry out, a method. Here the programmer would write the string variable, then a period, then the method. This could be saved as another

variable or it could be placed directly into an alert. One method that

This page says:

THIS IS MY STRING

OK

can be used on strings is *toUpperCase( ).* This returns the same string in all CAPS. Notice that this method does not have anything in the parentheses:

var stringVar = "this is my string";
alert(stringVar.toUpperCase( ));

Similarly, there is
a way to return
the length of a
string. *.length* is
the way to return
the number of

This page says:
19
☐ Prevent this page from creating additional dialogs.
OK

characters in a string. Recall that a character is anything inside the
string, including numbers, letters, symbols, and even the spacebar.
This can be called the same way that the *toUpperCase( )* method
was, and again it can be stored as a variable or placed right into an
alert. Below is an example of finding the length of a greeting:

var greeting = ("hello, how are you?");
alert(greeting.length);

Here is a project that combines all the concepts learned thus far:

```
<script>
var greeting = "Hello";
var firstName = prompt("What is your first name?");
var lastName = prompt("What is your last name?");
var nameLength = firstName.length + lastName.length;
alert(greeting + " " + firstName.toUpperCase( ) + " " +
lastName.toUpperCase( ));
alert("By the way, you have " + nameLength + " letters in your
name");
</script>
```

Math methods

To use one of the Math methods, or any method, the object must be called upon first. If the programmer wants to use the *round* method, he or she would have to first say **Math** (the object) then use a period to separate the object and the method. Together it would look like this: ***Math.round(3.1415);***

Here is a list of a few Math methods, more can be found in the appendix:

round(numVar **);**	Rounds to the nearest integer
ceil(numVar **);**	Rounds up to the nearest integer
floor(numVar **);**	Rounds down to the nearest integer
abs(numVar **);**	Returns the absolute value
sqrt(numVar **);**	Finds the square root of the number
pow(numVar, numVar **);**	Raises the 1st # to the 2nd #'s power
min(numVar, numVar, ... **);**	Returns the lowest of the numbers
max(numVar, numVar, ... **);**	Returns the highest of the numbers
random( );	Returns a random number between 0 and 1

Notice the *random* method returns a number between 0 and 1. Since this will not be very helpful, an integer between 1 and 10 might be more logical. To do this, some math needs to be performed on the new number. First, multiply the random number by 10. Now it is a random number between 0 and 10 (still not an integer). Next, take the floor of the number—this makes the number an integer from 0 – 9. Finally, add 1 to the number to make it be between 1 and 10. These steps can be combined into one:

Math.floor(Math.random( )*10) + 1;

Notice that the order of operations does matter here. To change how many random numbers there can be, simply change what .random( ) is being multiplied by and to change the first number, add the new starting number where the 1 is.

Date Object

The Date object is a little different than the Math object in that it cannot be used by simply saying the name of the object; it is more like a String object, since the object should be stored in a variable. In the string object the assignment operator was all that need to be used; this is not the case in the Date object. The keyword *new* is used to assign a new instance of an object to a variable. When setting up a new instance of an object the name of the object followed by a set of parenthesis, usually empty, come after the *new* keyword. So, to store all the information of the date object in a variable called **d**, it would look like this:

var d = new Date( );

Now to use the methods that are associated with the Date object, use the dot operator between the variable and the method:

var month = d.getMonth( )

This will store the number of the month in a variable called *month*. The only problem with this is that it stores a number from 0-11, January being 0 and December being 11. A simple switch statement can fix this to display the correct month number or name. Similar steps also need to be taken for the day of the week and hour of the day.

An example of the code to make the date print out properly is on the following pages.

The Date Object - Displaying Date and Time

```
<script>
var date = new Date();
var dom = date.getDate();
var dow = date.getDay();
var month = date.getMonth();
var year = date.getFullYear();        Create
variable at
var mins = date.getMinutes();        the top of
code
var hour = date.getHours();
var amPm = "a.m.";

switch(dow)
{
    case 0: dow = "Sunday"; break;
    case 1: dow = "Monday"; break;
    case 2: dow = "Tuesday"; break;
    case 3: dow = "Wednesday"; break;
    case 4: dow = "Thursday"; break;
    case 5: dow = "Friday"; break;
    case 6: dow = "Saturday"; break;
}
```

```
switch(month)
{
    case 0: month = "January"; break;
    case 1: month = "February"; break;
    case 2: month = "March"; break;
    case 3: month = "April"; break;
    case 4: month = "May"; break;
    case 5: month = "June"; break;
    case 6: month = "July"; break;
    case 7: month = "August"; break;
    case 8: month = "September"; break;
    case 9: month = "October"; break;
    case 10: month = "November"; break;
    case 11: month = "December"; break;
}

if(hour >=  12)
{
    hour = hour -12;
    amPm = "p.m.";
}

if(hour = = 0)
    hour = 12;

if(mins<10)
```

```
    mins = "0" + mins;



alert("Today is " + dow + ", " + month + " "
+ dom + ", " +
    year + ". The time is " + hour + ":" +
mins + " " + amPm);

</script>
```

Arrays

As the programs begin to get more complex, more variables will be needed. An easy way to keep these variables neatly organized is with arrays. Programmers can create their own arrays and place whatever they want into them. Once an array is populated, more elements can be added without problems (unlike other languages).

The first step is to create the array, name it, and tell it how large it should be. The array itself is just another variable, so it looks just like setting up any other variable. After naming the array, use brackets to define an empty array:

>*var arrayName = [ ];*

Now you have created an array with nothing in it, now each element can be defined:

>*arrayName[0] = "something";*
>*arrayName[1] = "stuff";*

Remember that an array of size 2 has elements 0 and 1. In JavaScript, it is okay to add more elements than the size of the array; it will simply make the array one element larger. Another way to do the same thing would be to add all the elements when the array is being created. Instead of putting empty brackets, just put the desired contents of the array in the brackets:

var arrayName= ["something", "stuff",...];

Since arrays are objects, they contain properties and methods. An important property of arrays is **.length**. Like in String objects, length returns the number of items in object. The first index in an array is 0, so the last is always one less than total number of elements in the array. This can be written as **arrayName.length-1;**

This is also useful if an element needs to be added to the end of an array and the exact size is unknown or the size has changed. Since the last element in an array is length-1, the next element added would be at length. This can be written as:

arrayName[arrayName.length] = someValue;

The length also is used when using a loop to run through every element in an array. A for loop starting at 0 and ending at the arrays length-1 is best suited for array. The following code will add someValue to every element in arrayName, regardless of the size of the array.

```
for( var i = 0; i < arrayName.length; i++ )
    {
        arrayName[ i ] = someValue;
    }
```

Arrays also have methods that can be useful in many situations and save time by not having to write the code to perform these tasks. The **.sort( )** and **.reverse( )** methods are examples. Sort arranges the elements in alphabetical and reverse flips the order of the elements in the array. These could also be used together to first alphabetize the array and then flip it so the elements store in reverse alphabetical order, like this:

var newArray = arrayName.sort( ).reverse( );

Other useful methods can be found in the appendix and can do things like combine multiple arrays, add or subtract elements to the beginning or end of the array while shifting the other elements over, remove only elements that have certain values, and many more.

Searches

Arrays can hold a large list of data and it is useful to be able to search through the entire list to see if it contains certain values. Two popular search methods are the linear search and the binary search.

A **linear search** starts are the beginning of the list and checks every element of the list one by one until it finds the item that is being searched for. This is a simple algorithm to write and is extremely fast is the list is small or if the item is near the beginning of the list. If the list is long and the item is not in the list or it is near the end, it can be "expensive", meaning it cost a lot of memory space. Another positive of the linear search is that the list does not need to be in order.

A **binary search** is more like a game of higher or lower. If 50 was guessed when trying to guess a number between 1-100 and the number was lower, then it is known that the number cannot be in the range 50-100. This cuts the possible solutions in half. If 25 was guessed next and it was too low, then the range is cut in half again to 26-49. A binary search does the same thing, so to use it, the list must already be sorted. Binary searches are usually less expensive than linear searches, especially when the data sets are large, but sorting these first can be expensive. So, there are trade-off between the linear search and the binary search.

Functions

There will be times when certain blocks of code might be used in different places in the program. Instead of rewriting this code multiple times, a function can be created. A function is like a method, except the programmer sets up exactly what happens when a function runs. The best place to put these functions is in the head of the HTML file. To create a function, simply write the word *function* followed by what you want to name the function. Make sure there are not any other methods or key words that use that name in JavaScript. The name is followed by parentheses, which can be used to accept parameters. The function is then opened like loops or if statements, with a brace. Inside the function there can be as much or as little code as necessary. The function ends with a return statement and a closing brace. The return statement is followed by whatever needs to be sent back to the place where the function was called. For functions that do not need to return anything, simply write the word **return;** followed by a semicolon or leave it out altogether. The function will automatically return with no value when it hits the closing brace

> *function nameTheFunc( )*
> *{*
>> *//as much code as needed...*
>> *return someValue;(optional if nothing is being*
> *returned)*
>> *}*

Now that the function is created, it can be used as many times as desired by simply using the line: *nameTheFunc( );* or whatever the programmer named it.

function myFunc( )
    {
        var firstName = "Bob";
        var lastName = "Smith";
        return firstName + lastName;
    }

Like methods, functions can also take one or more parameter. Simply name these in the parenthesis and separate them by commas, if needed. A local copy of that variable can then be used anywhere inside of the function.

function anotherFunc(firstName, lastName)
    {
        var fullName = firstName + " " + lastName;
        return lastName;
    }

Note: all the variables in this example are considered local and can only be used inside of this function. If fullName is used outside of this function, then an error will occur (unless there is another local variable somewhere with the same name). This can be avoided using a global variable that all the code can see. To make a variable global, just define it at the top to the JavaScript, above any functions.

var fullName;

function anotherFunc(firstName, lastName)

{

      fullName = firstName + " " + lastName;

      return lastName;

}

The only difference in these two examples is var fullName is defined as a variable before the function, therefore the var fullName in the function is not needed. This way any function in the document can use and modify the variable fullName.

Events

Events are like messages or flags that objects can use to tell each other their state. The events looked at here will be the events that tell when an action, such as clicking a button or moving the mouse over a picture, is performed by the user. Events are used as attributes of HTML tags where they allow the programmer to run one line of JavaScript. There are many events, but the ones that will be most useful now are *onclick, onmouseover, onmouseout,* and *ondblclick.*

The most common of these is the *onclick* event, which will run one line of code when added to a button (or picture, any tag will work). Remember that this event is in the HTML code, not the JavaScript! In other words, the programmer must manually go into the code and find where the button is located. The easiest way to do this is by using the split view in the HTML editor that is being used; when the button is clicked, it should highlight the HTML code for the button. Now, at the end of that opening tag (before the >) add the line *onclick = "yourFunction( )"*.

This event should still be inside the tag:

<input type = "button" ... onclick = "yourFunction( )" >

Remember that this tag already exists if a button has been added; there is no need to write it out again. The other three events work in much the same way—the only difference is that *ondblclick* will run the code if the button is double clicked. *onmouseover* and *onmouseout* will run the code when the mouse hovers over the button and when the mouse leaves the button respectively. It is okay to have more than one event on one button, such as *onmouseover* and *onmouseout*.

Document Object

The document object is automatically loaded when the HTML file is opened in a browser and is named **document**. A useful method in the document object is *getElementById(str);* This method uses the id attribute of any HTML tags in the document. For example, if there was an image with the id: *myPicture*, it could be accessed using the following code:

document.getElementById("myPicture");

Element Objects

Element objects refer to the HTML elements within the document. Some elements are body, h1, p, input, etc., and are also called tags. These elements are typically referred to by their unique ID, like in the method **getElementById( )** from above. One important property of events is **innerHTML**. This property refers to the text in-between the opening and closing tags of an element. In the HTML code: **<h1 id="myH1"> My Heading </h1>** the innerHTML is "My Heading". Depending on what side of the assignment operator this property is on, it can either read or write to the document.

document.getElementById("myH1").innerHTML =
"I Just Changed My Heading";

The h1 would change from **My Heading** to **I Just Changed My Heading** in the example above. To save the current text in the h1 tag with the id of myH1 in a variable, the innerHTML would be on the right side of the assignment operator.

The following example show this.

var textInH1 = document.getElementById("myH1").innerHTML;

Note: If there is text already existing in the innerHTML (like in the 1st example) and a value is assigned to it, then it will replace that text.

Forms

Another reason functions are a great tool is because when events are used, only one line of code can be used. Using functions can change hundreds of lines of code to just one. In HTML, forms are employed when using items such as text boxes, text areas, check boxes, radio buttons, select (dropdown) boxes, buttons, and many other useful tools. Now, using JavaScript, some functionality can be added to these things. The most important thing here is being able to tell the code that a button has been pressed (like a submit button or an enter button). This is one place where the events come into play.

Form Options

Besides buttons, other items, such as radio buttons, check boxes, select boxes, and text areas, can also go into forms. The programmer needs to make sure these items are in the forms and that the forms are named with an ID. It would be simpler if there was only one form in any given page. To name a form, just add an id attribute to the tag remembering that this is case-sensitive. Most editors will automatically give forms and form elements a default ID, make sure to check the tag so there are not two id attributes.

Radio buttons, check boxes, select boxes, and text areas are just a few form elements, but without JavaScript they do not have any functionality. Using JavaScript, these buttons, boxes, and text areas can be used to get information from the webpage. Like forms, these items all need to be named so the programmer can reference them later using their id attributes. Most of these elements are automatically named when they are inserted.

Once the forms and fields are all named with id's, functions can be created in JavaScript to add functionality. In most cases, something will happen if one of the **checkboxes** is checked. For example, the function might add to a total if the user is purchasing something. For this type of function, an *if* statement could be used. First, tell the computer to look at the document that is open. Next, tell the computer what element is being evaluated by using **getElementById( )**. Now that the computer knows what it is looking at, ask the computer if that box is checked or not. If the box is checked, the computer will return true, and it will return false if the box is unchecked. An *if* statement would look something like this:

```
if( document.getElementById("checkbox").checked)
    {
            //do this if the box is checked...
            //.checked returns true of false so no need to
            //write == true
    }
```

Radio buttons are like checkboxes except for one major difference, radio buttons are all linked together. In other words, when one radio button is checked, no other button can be. To keep the radio buttons connected, they are stored in an **array**. If five radio buttons are added, then they will probably all be named something like R1. R1 is the name of the array; each button will be stored as elements in that array starting at zero. To call on an element, square brackets are used [ ]. The names of the first three radio buttons would be **R1[0]**, **R1[1]**, and **R1[2]**, to show this in an ID they would be **R1_0, R1_1,** and **R1_2.** If there are five buttons, the highest element would be 4 because they start at zero. The *if* statement for a radio button would look like this:

```
if( document.getElementById("R1_0").checked )
{
        //do this if the box is checked...
}
```

Select (dropdown) boxes are like radio buttons in that they are saved in an array. The dropdown box itself is the array, and each option is an element. One attribute about select boxes is selected, which can be true or false and by using the method **.selectedIndex** the index of the element that is currently selected (it will return -1 if nothing is selected) will be returned. To call attributes about the individual options, such as the value, the **.option** property is used, but in most case simply using the **.value** property on the array will be enough:

document.getElementById("select").value;

.value returns the value of the element selected. The values of each element need to be put in the array adding an attribute or using the property pallet in an editor.

In some cases, information might need to be retrieved or sent to a **text field**. To do this, simply assign a value to the text field or assign the text field to a new variable. Remember that whatever is on the left-hand side of the equal sign is what is being assigned a value. To save what is in the text field, type something along the lines of:

var stuff = document.getElementById("textfield").value;

To put something into the text area:

document.getElementById("textfield").value = "This will show up in the text area!";

Important Vocabulary

- **AND** – basic logic gate where every part of a statement must be true for the entire statement to be true
- **Constant** – used in coding to store a value that cannot be changed
- **Debugging** – finding errors in code
- **Design – Implement – Test** – the three steps of the iterative development process
- **Incremental** – done in small chunks
- **Iterative** – continuously repeats steps, in programming it uses loops
- **OR** – basic logic gate where any part of a statement can be true for the entire statement to be true
- **Selection** – the logic structure in programming that uses if statements to select certain values
- **Sequence** – the structure that runs one line after another
- **Variable** – used in coding to store a value that can change

Unit 9 – AP® Performance Task: Explore

Overview

Computing innovations impact our lives in ways that require considerable study and reflection for us to fully understand them. In this Performance Task, you will explore a computing innovation of your choice. Your close examination of this computing innovation will deepen your understanding of computer science principles.

You will be provided with 8 hours of class time to develop, complete, and submit the following:

- Computational Artifact
- Written Responses

General Requirements

This performance task requires you to select and investigate a computational innovation that:

- Has or has had the potential to have significant beneficial and harmful effects on society, economy, or culture.
- Consumes, produces, and/or transforms data.
- Raises at least one data storage concern, data privacy concern, or data security concern.

You are required to:

- Investigate your computing innovation using a variety of sources (e.g. print, online, expert interviews).

- Cite at least three sources that helped you create your computational artifact and/or formulate your written responses.

  o At least two of the sources must be available online or in print; your third source may be either online, in print, or a personal interview with an expert on the computing innovation.

  o At least two of the sources must have been created after the end of the previous academic year.

- Produce a computational artifact that illustrates, represents or explains the computing innovation's intended purpose, its function, or its effect.

- Provide written responses to questions about your computational artifact and computing innovation.

Submission Guidelines

1. Computational Artifact

Your computational artifact must provide an illustration, representation, or explanation of the computing innovation's intended purpose, its function, or its effect. The computational artifact must not simply repeat the information supplied in the written responses and should be primarily non-textual.

Submit a video, audio, or PDF file. Use computing tools and techniques to create one original computational artifact (a visualization, a graphic, a video, a program, or an audio recording). **Acceptable multimedia file types include .mp3, .mp4, .wmv, .avi, .mov, .wav, .aif, or .pdf format. PDFs must not exceed three pages. Video or audio files must not exceed 1 minute in length and must not exceed 30MB in size.**

2. Written Responses

Submit one PDF file in which you respond directly to each of the prompts below. **Clearly label your responses 2a–2e in order.** Your responses must provide evidence of the extensive knowledge you have developed about your chosen computing innovation and its impact(s). Write your responses so they would be understandable to someone who is not familiar with the computing innovation. Include citations, as applicable, within your written responses. **Your response to prompts 2a–2d combined must not exceed 700 words.** The references required in 2e are not included in the final word count.

2a. Provide information on your computing innovation and computational artifact.

- Name the computing innovation that is represented by your computational artifact.
- Describe the computing innovation's intended purpose and function.
- Describe how your computational artifact illustrates, represents, or explains the computing innovation's intended purpose, its function, or its effect.

(Approximately 100 words)

2b. Describe your development process, explicitly identifying the computing tools and techniques you used to create your artifact. Your description must be detailed enough so that a person unfamiliar with those tools and techniques will understand your process.

(Approximately 100 words)

Computing Innovation

2c. Explain at least one beneficial effect and at least one harmful effect the computing innovation has had, or has the potential to have, on society, economy, or culture.

(Approximately 250 words)

2d. Using specific details, describe:

- the data your innovation uses;
- how the innovation consumes (as input), produces (as output), and/or transforms data; and
- at least one data storage concern, data privacy concern, or data security concern directly related to the computing innovation.

(Approximately 250 words)

References

2e. Provide a list of at least three online or print sources used to create your computational artifact and/or support your responses to the prompts provided in this performance task.

- At least two of the sources must have been created after the end of the previous academic year.

- For each online source, include the permanent URL. Identify the author, title, source, the date you retrieved the source, and, if possible, the date the reference was written or posted.
- For each print source, include the author, title of excerpt/article and magazine or book, page number(s), publisher, and date of publication.
- If you include an interview source, include the name of the person you interviewed, the date on which the interview occurred, and the person's position in the field.
- Include citations for the sources you used, and number each source accordingly.
- Each source must be relevant, credible, and easily accessed.

Scoring Guidelines

The Explore Performance Task will be evaluated based upon the 7 discrete criteria listed below. Each criterion is scored individually on a binary scale (i.e., each criterion can earn a score of 1 or 0) for a total of 7 possible points.

The first criterion is evaluated based upon the computational artifact, using the written response as needed. The remaining six criteria are evaluated based upon the written response.

Computational Artifact and Written Response (1, 2a, and 2b, approximately 200 words)

1) **Using Development Processes and Tools:** The computational artifact identifies the **computing innovation** and provides an illustration, representation, or explanation of the computing innovation's intended purpose, function, or effect.

Written Response (2c)

2) **Analyzing Impact of Computing:** States a plausible fact about **the computing innovation's** intended purpose or function.

3) **Analyzing Impact of Computing:** Identifies at least ONE effect of the **computing innovation.**

4) **Analyzing Impact of Computing:** Identifies a beneficial effect AND a harmful effect of the **computing innovation.** Explains how ONE of the identified effects impacts or has the potential to impact society, economy, or culture.

Written Response (2d)

5) **Analyzing Data and Information:** Identifies the data that the **computing innovation** uses. Explains how that data is consumed, produced, OR transformed.

6) **Analyzing Data and Information**: Identifies one storage, privacy, OR security concern. Explains how the concern is related to the **computing innovation**.

Written Response (2e)

7) **Finding and Evaluating Information**: Provides inline citations (APA format) of at least 3 attributed sources within the written response. The citations must be used to justify the response.

Source: AP Computer Science Principles Course Description
Copyright © 2016 The College Board.
Reproduced with permission.
http://apcentral.collegeboard.com.

Unit 10 – AP® Performance Task: Create

Overview

Programming is a collaborative and creative process that brings ideas to life through the development of software. Programs can help solve problems, enable innovations, or express personal interests. In this Performance Task, you will be developing a program of your choice. Your development process should include iteratively designing, implementing, and testing your program.

You will be provided with 12 hours of class time to complete and submit the following:

- A video of your program running
- Written responses about your program and development process
- Program Code

General Requirements

This performance task requires you to develop a program on a topic that interests you or one that solves a problem. It is strongly recommended that a portion of the program involve some form of collaboration with another student in your class. Your program development process must involve a significant portion of work completed independently that requires a significant level of planning, designing, and program development.

You are required to:

- Iteratively design, implement, and test your program.
- Independently create at least one significant part of your program.
- Create a video that displays the running of your program and demonstrates its functionality.
- Write responses to questions about your program.
- Include your entire program code.
- Program Requirements

Your program must demonstrate a variety of capabilities and implement several different language features that, when combined, produce a result that cannot easily be accomplished without computing tools and techniques. Your program should draw upon a combination of mathematical and logical concepts, such as use of numbers, variables, mathematical expressions with arithmetic operators, logical and Boolean operators and expressions, decision statements, iteration, and collections.

Submission Guidelines

1. Video

Submit one video in .mp4, .wmv, .avi, or .mov format that demonstrates the running of at least one significant feature of your program. **Your video must not exceed 1 minute in length and must not exceed 30MB in size.**

2. Written Responses

Submit one PDF file in which you respond directly to each prompt. **Clearly label your responses 2a–2d in order. Your response to all prompts combined must not exceed 750 words, exclusive of the Program Code.**

Program Purpose and Development

2a. Provide a written response or audio narration in your video that:

- identifies the programming language;
- identifies the purpose of your program; and
- explains what the video illustrates.

(Approximately 150 words)

2b. Describe the incremental and iterative development process of your program, focusing on two distinct points in that process. Describe the difficulties and/or opportunities you encountered and how they were resolved or incorporated. In your description clearly indicate whether the development described was collaborative or independent. At least one of these points must refer to independent program development.

(Approximately 200 words)

2c. Capture and paste the program code segment that implements an algorithm (marked with an oval in section 3 below) that is fundamental for your program to achieve its intended purpose. Your code segment must include an algorithm that integrates other algorithms and integrates mathematical and/or logical concepts. Describe how each algorithm within your selected algorithm functions independently, as well as in combination with others, to form a new algorithm that helps to achieve the intended purpose of the program.

(Approximately 200 words)

2d. Capture and paste the program code segment that contains an abstraction you developed (marked with a rectangle in section 3 below). Your abstraction should integrate mathematical and logical concepts. Explain how your abstraction helped manage the complexity of your program.

(Approximately 200 words)

3. Program Code

Capture and paste your entire program code in this section.

- Mark with an **oval** the segment of program code that implements the algorithm you created for your program that integrates other algorithms and integrates mathematical and /or logical concepts.
- Mark with a **rectangle** the segment of program code that represents an abstraction you developed.
- Include comments or citations for program code that has been written by someone else.

High Quality Submissions will:

1, 2a. The video demonstrates the running of at least one feature of the program that illustrates the program's intended purpose as described in the written response or the video narration.

2b. The response describes a difficulty and an opportunity encountered (or two difficulties or two opportunities) at two points in the development of the program.

AND

The response describes how each of the difficulties and/or opportunities were resolved and incorporated as part of an **incremental and iterative development process.**

AND

The response must identify at least one point in the development of the program that was completed **independently.**

2c. The selected algorithm integrates two or more commonly used or new algorithms, and integrates mathematical and/or logical concepts to create a new algorithm.

AND

The response identifies the algorithm's purpose in the program and accurately describes with specificity how the algorithm achieves this purpose.

AND

The response accurately describes how two of the algorithms function independently as well as in combination to create a new algorithm.

If needed, more than one area of the program code can be selected as part of the response to describe the algorithm.

2d. The selected abstraction integrates mathematical and/or logical concepts and serves to manage complexity of the program.

AND

The response indicates that an abstraction was developed and provides an accurate description with specificity of the purpose of the abstraction.

AND

The response explains how the abstraction manages complexity of the program due to the inclusion of the abstraction in the program or explains how the program would function without the abstraction.

When necessary, the response should include descriptions of a list(s) or procedure(s), and explains any use of parameters and return values in the abstraction.

**If needed, more than one area of the program code can be selected as part of the response to describe the abstraction.

Appendix

String Object

var *youVar* = "a string";

yourVar.METHOD( );

String Object Properties

Property	Description
length	Returns the number of **characters** in the string

String Object Methods

Method	Description
toUpperCase( )	Returns the string in all uppercase letters
toLowerCase( )	Returns the string in all lowercase letters
charAt(int)	Returns what character is at the specified index
substring(int1, int2)	Returns the string from index **int1** to

	index **int2** -1
substring(int)	Returns the string from index **int** to the last character of the string
concat(str1, str2, str3, …)	Combines two or more stings together
sup( )	Changes the string into a superscript
sub( )	Changes the string into a subscript
parseInt(str)	Changes the string into an integer
parseFloat(str)	Changes the string into a floating-point number (decimal)

Math Object

Math.METHOD( );

Math Object Properties

Property	Description
E	Returns Euler's constant (approx. 2.718)
LN2	Returns the natural logarithm of 2 (approx. 0.693)
LN10	Returns the natural logarithm of 10 (approx. 2.302)
LOG2E	Returns the base-2 logarithm of E (approx. 1.414)
LOG10E	Returns the base-10 logarithm of E (approx. 0.434)
PI	Returns PI (approx. 3.14159)
SQRT1_2	Returns the square root of 1/2 (approx. 0.707)
SQRT2	Returns the square root of 2 (approx. 1.414)

Math Object Methods

Method	Description

abs(num)	Returns the absolute value of a number
ceil(num)	Returns the value of a number rounded upwards to the nearest integer
floor(num)	Returns the value of a number rounded downwards to the nearest integer
round(num)	Rounds a number to the nearest integer
min(num1, num2, ...)	Returns the number with the lowest value of x and y
max(num1, num2, ...)	Returns the number with the highest value of x and y
sqrt(num)	Returns the square root of a number
pow(num, num)	Returns the value of x to the power of y
random( )	Returns a random number between 0 and 1 (excluding 1)

sin(num)	Returns the sine of a number
cos(num)	Returns the cosine of a number
tan(num)	Returns the tangent of an angle

Document & HTML Objects

document.METHOD( );

Document Object Properties

Property	Description
bgColor	Sets or returns the color of the background
fgColor	Sets or returns the color of the foreground
title	Returns the title of the current document
cookie	Sets or returns all cookies associated with the current document
domain	Returns the domain name for the current document
lastModified	Returns the date and time a document was last modified
referrer	Returns the URL of the document that loaded the current document
URL	Returns the URL of the current document

Document Object Methods

Method	Description
getElementById("*id*")	Returns the element of a specific HTML tag using specified ID

Element Object Properties

innerHTML	Sets text in between the opening and closing of specific HTML tags
style	Sets or returns the value of the style attribute of an element
className	Sets or returns the value of the class attribute of an element

Document Object Methods

blur( )	Takes focus off the element
focus( )	Gives focus to the element
click( )	Simulates a mouse click on the element

Date Object

var *yourObj* = new Date( );

var *newVar* = *yourObj*.*METHOD*( );

Date Methods

Method	Description
Date( )	Returns today's date and time
getDate( )	Returns the day of the month from a Date object (from 1-31)
getDay( )	Returns the day of the week from a Date object (from 0-6)
getMonth( )	Returns the month from a Date object (from 0-11)
getFullYear( )	Returns the year, as a four-digit number, from a Date object
getHours( )	Returns the hour of a Date object (from 0-23)
getMinutes( )	Returns the minutes of a Date object (from 0-59)
getSeconds( )	Returns the seconds of a Date object (from 0-59)

getMilliseconds( )	Returns the milliseconds of a Date object (from 0-999)
getTime( )	Returns the number of milliseconds since midnight Jan 1, 1970. Also, known as Internet Time.

Array Object

var *yourArray* = [ ];

yourArray[0] = *something*;

yourArray[1] = *somethingElse*;

...

yourArray.METHOD( );

Array Object Properties

Property	Description
length	Returns the number of elements in the array

Array Object Methods

Method	Description
concat(A_1, A_2,...)	Combines two or more arrays and returns an array
reverse( )	Reverses the order of the array and returns an array

join(str)	Changes the array into a string and separates them with the specified string and returns a string
sort( )	Rearranges the array in alphabetical or numerical order and returns an array
push( )	Adds new elements to the end of an array, and returns the new length
pop( )	Removes the last element of an array, and returns that element
shift( )	Removes the first element of an array, and returns that element
unshift( )	Adds new elements to the beginning of an array, and returns the new length
splice(num and/or **str)**	Adds/Removes elements from an array
slice(int1 , int2)	Selects a part of an array, and returns the new array from index **int1** to index **int2-1**

Events

Place the event followed by an equal sign and a function inside of an HTML tag.

<SOMETAG ... anEvent = "yourFunction( )">

Event	Description
onclick	When the mouse is clicked
ondblclick	When the mouse is double clicked
onkeypress	When a key on the keyboard is pressed
onkeydown	When a key on the keyboard is pressed down
onkeyup	When a key on the keyboard is released
onload	When the page is loaded
onreset	When the refresh button is pressed
onresize	When the page is resized
onselect	When text on the page is selected
onsubmit	When the submit button is

	pressed
onunload	When the page is closed
onmouseover	When the mouse is over the element
onmouseout	When the mouse is taken off an element
onmouseup	When the mouse button is released
onmousedown	When the mouse button is pressed down
onmousemove	When the mouse moves
onerror	When an error occurs on the page

List of Useful HTML5 Tags

template – used in every html file:

<!doctype html>

<html>

<head>

<meta charset="UTF-8">

<title>...</title>

</head>

<body>

...

</body>

</html>

       id   - all tags. gives a unique identification to the tag

---

<head>...</head>   - tells where the head starts and finishes

<title>...</title>   - title in the document window title bar

---

<body>   - tells where the body of the website starts

text   - changes the color of all text in file

bgcolor   - changes the color of the background

background   - inserts an image as the background

link   - changes the color of unvisited links

vlink   - changes the color of visited links

\<p\>...\</p\>   - paragraph

    align   - aligns the paragraph left, right, or centered

\<h1\>...\</h1\>   - heading #1(largest)

...

\<h6\>...\</h6\>   - heading #6(smallest)

\<ol\>   - ordered list

    \<li\>   - list items

    ...

    \<li\>

\</ol\>

```
<ul>                          - unordered list (bullet points)
    <li>                      - list item
    ...
    </li>
</ul>
```

```
<dl>                          - definition list
    <dt>                      - definition term
    <dd>                      - definition description
</dl>
```

```
<br />                        - break
    clear = left(right)       - aligns text back after
                                  wrapping around an image
<nobr>...</nobr>              - will not let a line break
```

```
<center>...</center>  - centers heading, paragraphs, images, etc.
```

```
<pre>...</pre>                - enter preformatted text
```

`<!-- ... -->`   - enter a comment

`<b>...</b>`   - bold

`<i> ...</i>`   - italicize

`<u>...</u>`   - underline

`<strike>... </strike>`   - strikethrough text

`<sup>...</sup>`   - superscript

`<sub>... </sub>`   - subscript

`<big>...</big>`   - enlarges text size

< small>... </small>   - decreases text size

<tt>...</tt>   - typewriter text

<font>...</font>

    face   - changes font

    size   - changes font size

    color   - changes font color

---

                                                                                                                                                            nbsp   - inserts a blank space into your text

    &#___   - inserts a special character into your text

<img>   - image tag

    src   - defines the source of the image

    alt   - gives an alternative name for the
picture

    align   - aligns for wrapped text (right/left,
top/middle/bottom)

    border   - adds a border to image (zero for
none)

    vspace   - adds vertical space next to picture

    hspace   - adds horizontal space between picture

height	- sets the height of the picture
width	- sets the width of the picture

(note: if only height or width is used, the picture will stay proportional.)

<hr>	- adds a horizontal rule
size	- sets thickness of rule
width	- sets width of rule (use %)
align	- aligns left, center, or right

<a>...</a>	- link
href	- location to direct link
name	- names a webpage area displayed by link
target	- specifies where a link opens (i.e.- _blank)

<meta name="copyright" content="?">
<meta name="author" content="?">
<meta name="keywords" content="?">
<meta name="description" content="?">
<meta name="robots" content="?">

Important Vocabulary for the AP®
Computer Science Principles Test

AND – basic logic gate where every part of a statement must be true for the entire statement to be true

Applications – includes word processors, photo editing software, web browsers, games, music programs, almost everything else on the computer excluding saved files

ARPANET – the Advanced Research Projects Agency Network, first agency to use TCP/IP

ASCII – American Standard Code for Information Interchange

Asymmetric key encryption – a different key is used to encrypt and decrypt a message

Bandwidth – the amount of recourses available to transmit the data

Big Data – sets of data that are larger than a consumer software application can handle

Binary – base 2, number system that uses 0, 1

Bit – each number in the binary system, 0 or 1

Bit Rate – the number of bits that can be processed per second

Byte – 8 bits

Caesar Cipher – a shift cipher where each letter is shifted the same amount

Central Processing Unit (CPU) – carries out every command or process on the computer and can be thought of as the brain of the computer

Cipher – is a pair of algorithms that give details on how to encrypt and decrypt the data

Client – any computer that requests a service

Cloud Computing – using a remote server to store files

CMYK – used for printing and stands for **C**yan, **M**agenta, **Y**ellow, and Black (**Key**) where the number associated with each letter is the percent of each color used

Computationally hard – a problem that even a computer would take too long to find the exact solution

Computer – an electronic device that processes data according to a set of instructions or commands, known as a program

Constant – used in coding to store a value that cannot be changed

Core – the central processing unit (CPU) and the main memory

CSS – Cascading Style Sheets, redefines mark-up in HTML

DDoS – distributed denial-of-service attack, hackers flood a site with fake request making all the site's recourses unavailable for legitimate users

Debugging – finding errors in code

Decimal – base 10, number system that used 0-9

Decryption – the reverse process of encryption

Design – Implement – Test – the three steps of the iterative development process

Digit – each number in the decimal system, 0-9

Digital Certificate – a trusted third-party file that shows the site is verified and legit

Digital signature – an electronic signature that, by using public key, can be verified authentic

DNS – Domain Name System, one of the smaller networks that make up the Internet and contains many servers that act like phone books

Domain Name – a name given or linked to an IP address

Encryption – taking text and converting it so it is illegible

Fault Tolerant – a property of IP, if there is an error, it will still work properly

FTP – File Transfer Protocol, used for file transferring

Hacker – someone who exploits weaknesses on a computer or network and can steal or disrupt data

Hardware – the physical parts of the computer. Devices such as the monitor, keyboard, speakers, wires, chips, cables, plugs, disks, printers, mice, and many other

Heuristic approach – an approach that gives results that are "good enough" when an exact answer is not necessary.

Hexadecimal – base 16, number system that uses 0-9 and a-f

HTML – Hyper Text Markup Language, the standard for creating web pages

HTTP – Hyper Text Transfer Protocol, used for websites

HTTPS – a secure version of HTTP that uses SSL/TLS

IMAP – Internet Message Access Protocol, used for e-mail

Incremental – done in small chunks

Input and output (I/O) devices – how the user interacts with the computer

Internet – a network of smaller networks connected using a specific set of rules that computers use to communicate with each other

IP – Internet protocol, a unique address for every device connected to the Internet

IP Address – a unique identifier for every device on the Internet

IPv4 – the version of IP that uses 32-bit addresses

IPv6 – the version of IP that uses 128-bit addresses

ISP – Internet Service Provider

Iterative – continuously repeats steps, in programming it uses loops

Key – in cryptography, a shared secret to make the difficulty of the encryption harder to crack

Latency – the amount of delay when sending digital data over the Internet or the round-trip time information take to get from the client to the server and back

Lossless – a data compression that does not lose data during compression

Lossy – a data compression that loses data during compression

Main memory – memory that temporarily stores information while it is being sent to the CPU, also called RAM

Metadata – additional data about the main data, usually at the beginning of a file

Modular arithmetic – using the remainder when dividing, also known as clock arithmetic

Name Server – a server that contains many IP addresses and their matching domain names

Network – a group of computers that are connected so they can share resources using a data link

Nonvolatile – does not need a power supply, information is physically written to the device

Nybble (or Nibble) – half of a byte, 4 bits

One-way Function - a problem that is easy in one direction and difficult in the other

Operating System – the visual representation of the computer

OR – basic logic gate where any part of a statement can be true for the entire statement to be true

Packets – small chunks of data used in TCP/IP

Peripherals – the input and output (I/O) devices and the secondary memory

Phishing – using "bait" to trick the user into entering sensitive information like user names, passwords, or credit card numbers

Pixelation – when individual pixels are too large and the image begins to look blocky

POP – Post Office Protocol, used for e-mail

Private Key – a shared secret to help decrypt a message

Protocol – a specific set of rules

Public Key – a system that allows a key to be publicly published

Random Access Memory – memory that can be retrieved or written to anywhere without having to go through all the previous memory

RGB – stands for **Red, Green,** and **Blue** and refers to the color of light used in most monitors or screens

Root Name Server – one of 13 servers that contain every IP addresses and their matching domain names

Router – a networking device that routes Internet traffic to the destination

Sample rate – usually measured in bits per second, how often an analog signal is used when converting to digital

Secondary memory – used for long term storage and gets physically changed when files are saved or deleted

Selection – the logic structure in programming that uses if statements to select certain values

Sequence – the structure that runs one line after another

Sequential Memory – memory used to store back-up data on a tape

Server – any computer that provides a service

Software – a series of ones and zeros at the lowest level and cannot physically be touched and is usually stored on the hard drive of the computer and includes the operating system and the applications.

SSL – Secure Sockets Layer, issues digital certificates for websites

Subdomain – precedes the domain name, owned by the domain *https://subdomain.domain.com*

Substitution cipher – a cipher where a letter is mapped or swapped with another letter in the alphabet

Symmetric key encryption – the same key is used to encrypt and decrypt a message

TCP – Transmission Control Protocol, requests are broken down in to smaller, more manageable packets and numbered

TLS – Transport Layer Security, issues digital certificates for websites

UDP – User Datagram Protocol, like TCP and usually used for streaming audio/video

URL – Uniform Resource Locator, a specific file from a domain

Variable – used in coding to store a value that can change

Virus – a program that infects other programs and usually spreads to other programs or computers by copying itself repeatedly

VoIP – Voice over Internet Protocol, used for telephony

Volatile – needs a power supply, information is deleted when the power is turned off

Web (World Wide Web) – the part of the Internet that uses HTTP and HTTPS

Made in the USA
Lexington, KY
01 November 2017